CRANFORD PUBLIC LIBRARY N.J.
3 9520 00047 7812

Corporate Attractions

"*CORPORATE ATTRACTIONS* is a real and shocking story—but it is complete with solutions for every working person, especially managers."

Bernice Resnick Sandler
Executive Director
Project on the Status and Education of Women
Association of American Colleges

"A sad and powerful story . . . offers help for avoiding sexual harassment on the job."

Arthur Levine, Chairman
Institute for Educational Management
Harvard University

"*CORPORATE ATTRACTIONS* offers sound advice on a serious workplace problem which concerns the entire working world, particularly in employment areas where women are playing new roles."

General Jack N. Merritt, U.S. Army Retired
Executive Vice President
Association of the United States Army

"This compelling, gripping and honest story draws important lessons about the painful limits of the legal system's ability to redress sexual harassment, and about the urgent need for increased corporate education and sensitivity to the frequency and impact of the problem.

Neville's persepective as a victim of sexual harassment and as a plaintiff is one that has much to teach lawyers, law professors, judges, managers, and employees. Neville draws on her experience to offer sound, practical advice to employees and employers—advice that if followed should reduce the incidences of sexual harassment and make its aftermath less destructive for all involved."

Lucinda M. Finley
Professor of Law
SUNY/Buffalo Law School

Corporate Attractions

An Inside Account of Sexual Harassment with The New Sexual Rules for Men and Women on the Job

by Kathleen Neville

ACROPOLIS BOOKS LTD.
WASHINGTON, D.C.

"*CORPORATE ATTRACTIONS* is a practical book which will find its audience among potential plaintiffs and as a resource for lawyers in making legal presentations to clients."

Allen G. Siegle
Attorney at Law
Arent, Fox, Kintner, Plotkin & Kahn

"Many people are unclear as to what constitutes sexual impropriety in the workplace. Neville wants to purge those out-of-date guidelines."

Don Oldenburg
The Washington Post

"Kathleen Neville is putting her life back together after a grueling court battle that pitted her against her employer. She's also speaking out loud and clear about the sexual harassment problem in this country."

Louise Continelli
The Buffalo News

"In 1981 Neville was threatened with the loss of her job if she didn't sleep with her boss; she was fired when she complained to his superior. She sued, and the court ruled that there had been a quid pro quo instance of harassment, but that it was unrelated to the termination of her employment."

Savvy

The entity referred to as Channel 2 was owned and operated by a different company during the time this story took place and has nothing whatsoever to do with the present management or policies of the current Channel 2.

"Kathleen Neville's revealing account of her own experience shows the limits of the ability of courts and rules of law to control sexual harassment on the job. At the same time she has used the experience to develop steps that employers can put to immediate and practical use so as to avoid litigation and at the same time serve the ends that law suits simply cannot broadly reach."

Burke Marshall, Professor
Yale Law School

ACROPOLIS BOOKS, LTD.
11250-22 Roger Bacon Dr.
Reston, VA 22090

Library of Congress Cataloging-in-Publication Data
Neville, Kathleen, 1953-
Corporate attractions : the new rules for men and women on the job / Kathleen Neville.
p. cm.
ISBN 0-87491-952-5 : $19.95. —
ISBN 0-87491-953-3 (pbk.) : $12.95
1. Sex in the workplace. 2. Sexual harassment of women.
I. Title.
HF5549.5.S45N48 1990
331.4'133—dc20 89-17750
CIP

In memory of my father

and

to my mother

Table of Contents

Acknowledgments

Before I thank the people who assisted in this publication, I must first thank those individuals who helped me through the difficult experience that led me to write such a book.

I thank Louis Patack, Jim Meyerson, Jonathan Moore, JoAnne Breidenstein, Ralfa Musialowski, Diane Sciandra, Sandra Poulus-Swana, Andrea Brookman, Karen Parsons-Lansing, Sandee Lorenzo, Ken Slomovitz, Tom Brydges, the late Dr. John Argue, Paul LaMorticello and Dan O'Connell and staff for their courage, conviction and presence in the litigation process.

I am deeply indebted to friends who saw me through the "trial years" especially Elisabeth Attisano, Molly McCoy, Joyce and Joan Zoerb, Nancy Thon, Margaret Frischholz, Christye Peterson, Eileen Farrell, Lynn Sochon, Susan Painter, Robin Lenhart, Mr. and Mrs. Carlos, Mr. and Mrs. Riordan, Mr. and Mrs. Thomas Jackson, my friends at Shea's Buffalo Theater especially Barbara Maloney, Maureen Egan and Debbie Trimble, those at L. L. Berger's especially Mr. Louis L. Berger, Jr., WGR-TV, WBEN Radio, WIVB-TV, WKBW-TV and, in particular, *The Buffalo News* and other local organizations and companies in the western New York area who offered their support in special and different ways.

I thank all of my family—including my mother and brothers Timothy, James Patrick, William and Richard and all the members of the Neville/Sheedy/Connelly family. I especially thank a special member of our family, the late Reverend James Patrick Cahill, for his eternal support.

Thea Lango, it is impossible to thank you but I still need to try. I wouldn't have made it through the final lap without your help. And there aren't enough words of thanks to give my faith-filled friend, Donna Ent, for her continual and constant support during the "starting-over" process.

I would like to thank and remember the late Walter Hackl for believing in the importance and need for this book.

I wish to thank Acropolis Books Ltd. especially Al Hackl, Kathleen Hughes, John Hackl, Sandra Trupp, Joanna Shaw Eagle, Kathleen Cunningham, Judy Mollen, and a special thanks to my editor, Jean B. Bernard, whose sensitivity and understanding of the material meant a great deal to me.

I am deeply indebted to those who supported and encouraged this writing project. I wish to thank my "other" family Michael and Jackie Clark for their friendship and constant support and Sarah Ryan for her expert editorial advice and for believing in the book when it was only one page long. I also wish to thank John Davis, Priscilla Smith, Emily Hurst, Leslie Szejk, Steve Yale-Loehr, Melissa Pinder, Douglas Bates, James Fyock, Judith Pheiffer, Melinda Dillon, Mary Claycomb and Gary Ferris for their help and daily encouragement.

I am especially grateful to all the wonderfully supportive people in my hometown, Wilson, New York—

particularly the faculty and staff of Wilson High School including Mr. Stephen LaRock and Mr. Kenneth Voltz.

I am very grateful to the women and men who have shared their stories with me during the past eight years especially the members of WAGES in Washington, D.C.

I thank the family of the late Judge Daranco for allowing me to share the saddest moment in their lives with the hope that others will never have to experience such a loss.

And finally, my thanks to TK "Longfellow" who seems to have a knack for inspiring people to write books.

Foreword

Down the Rabbit Hole

"What do you know about this business?" the King said to Alice.
"Nothing," said Alice.
"Nothing, whatever?" persisted the King.
"Nothing whatever," said Alice.
"That's very important," the King said, turning to the jury.

Alice's Adventures in Wonderland
Lewis Carroll

Many caring people have said to me over the past few years that writing this book would be good for me. "Yes, by all means, write a book about it," friends nodded enthusiastically. "Then, at last, you can put that unfortunate incident' behind you." "It would be an excellent form of catharsis," they encouraged. And, surely, in some important ways, my well-meaning Aristotelian supporters are absolutely right: writing about something unpleasant and difficult that you have experienced does provide a desired cleansing effect.

Although catharsis might have provided a much needed spiritual benefit in bringing together the information found within these pages, that is not the real reason I've written this book. From my own experiences, and now as a counselor—and more often—confidante to the many working people experiencing problems resulting from men and women being together on the job, I began to realize that no easy-to-understand book existed that talked sensibly and directly to working people. No one was adequately warning people about and working them around the many "rabbit holes" found in the working world. I found legal manuals and company policy manuals, none of which clearly and satisfactorily answered the questions and concerns I had heard first from myself and then from countless others. It was more than apparent: People needed advice—good advice. And although many professionals are quick to recognize that men and women in the workplace face serious dilemmas, until now no one has seemed to come up with any solutions.

But even realizing the need for such a book was not reason enough to write one. And, of course, the even bigger question can be raised at this point as to why should I be the one to write it. After all, I was in television, not human resources, when I first experienced sexual harassment. I am a communicator, not a clinical psychologist or a labor lawyer. What do I know about all of this business?

I know a lot. I know what it feels like to be sexually harassed on the job—what it's like to be fired from a job for being involved (or refusing to be involved) with a supervisor. I have seen firsthand what office romances can do to a workplace. In fact, I had such a severe problem on the job that I had no choice but to take the hard road through the judicial system to find a solution. I didn't get my job back, but I survived and have gone on to find out how other people managed their personal dilemmas regarding the relationships between men and women on the job.

I have consulted the employment lawyers and human resource people and corporate managers and psychologists and psychiatrists and developed some solid commonsense advice for all of us who work. While some other sources are steering people to find love on the job and have it all and damn anyone who gets in your way, I am now able to offer better advice to others so that they will be spared what I was not. I speak to working people as though talking to someone sitting in the office right next door, like a trusted coworker and friend. I have discovered that working people don't want to hear just about legal cases; they want to hear about how the people *behind* those cases dealt with the problems they were forced to face.

Somewhere during a long and unplanned "fall down a rabbit hole" that took me on a journey I will never forget, I have become a specialist on a topic that unfortunately has chosen me as one of its examples. After more than seven years of struggling for answers to questions, and endless days and months of talking to human resource people and lawyers and behavioral scientists, I am more than able to answer those searching questions myself. Without intending to, I have become knowledgeable on something that, good or bad, completely changed the direction of my own life. And because of the dramatic effect on my life and career, I feel compelled to share my experience and knowledge about men and women on the job. By sharing my acquired knowledge of the possible rabbit holes all of us need to avoid, I offer the inside account and advice in this book with the great hope that what I have learned will make a difference to other working people. And, it is for those people that this book is written.

Kathleen Neville

Introduction

The Big Picture and the Big Problem

Intramural flings, trysts, courtships and marriages are becoming as much a way of life as pinstripe suits. In law firms as well as elsewhere, sex is a preoccupation; a professional issue. And, as more women join the ranks, a management problem.

New York Times
July 29, 1988

I speak from experience when I say working America has a problem on its hands.

The old unwritten guidelines regarding the social/sexual relationships men and women develop, pursue, or flee from while on the job no longer apply. And the problem is getting bigger every day. People are unclear as to what is or is not proper behavior between men and women at work. And until now no one has offered a new set of rules for men and women to follow.

Corporate Attractions is written for working people. Centered upon an actual inside account of sexual harassment, this book offers positive and understandable solutions to problems men and women face every day on the job. By offering basic rules as a guide, this text addresses the types of people and behavior we will all confront in our working lives. It offers ways in which we can deal with each person and situation we encounter in a positive manner. As working people are finding out, each of us needs to be responsible for the way we act—and react—to others while at work. Careers shouldn't be destroyed, jobs shouldn't be lost, and personal lives shouldn't be shattered because of the failure of both people and companies to respond properly to situations involving emotions and actions of men and women on the job.

The problem is very real, but, fortunately, so are the solutions.

The Facts and Figures

The figures about today's evolving workplace speak for themselves. Currently, more than 54 percent of our workforce is comprised of women. According to the Bureau of National Affairs, by the year 2000, more than 70 percent of new hires will be either women or other minorities. Labor statistics show that the proportion of women who are in the labor force has grown from one-third in 1950 to more than one-half today. Since 1970, nearly half of the increase in the female labor force has been among women age 25 to 34. According to the Bureau of Labor Statistics, today, one of four women workers is in this age group. These women join the ranks of approximately 65 million men.

And what makes all of this so interesting are the statistics and facts of *another* kind:

- Since 12.7 million people in managerial positions spend approximately 50 hours a week on the job and spend all but 29 hours a week either commuting or preparing to go to work, this (according to market research) brings the chances of men and women becoming involved with someone they meet through work to almost 75 percent.

- In a recent survey conducted on sexual harassment results showed that one in every three working women feels she is the victim of unwanted advances and is being sexually harassed on the job.

- The Merit Systems Protection Board reports that 42 percent of the women working for the federal government say they have been sexually harassed.

- In another recent study conducted by Northwest Missouri State University surveying both men and women, 46 percent of the men said they thought women should be flattered by what they agreed was the definition of sexual harassment.

- The most revealing survey released by *Working Woman* magazine in December 1988 shows that "nearly 90 percent of Fortune 500 companies have received complaints of sexual harassment; more than a third already have been hit with a lawsuit; nearly a quarter have been sued repeatedly."

- According to that same survey, since 1980 more than 38,500 sexual harassment cases have been filed with the federal government.

The New Environment

Obviously, the working world provides an explosive environment. How all these people get along with each other on the job is now a major concern of both individuals and the companies employing them. But there is hardly a simple, ready-made solution to this widespread and puzzling dilemma.

Experts on the topic of management and motivation agree that happy workers are more productive. In fact, they already knew that back in the 1950s heyday of B. F. Skinner. But the behavioral science experts didn't really ready their ship for the crew of working women who boarded the boat in the past two decades and are now helping to keep corporate America afloat. In all fairness to the experts, no one was truly ready for the rapid rise in the number of working women, nor for the good and bad relationships and costly conflicts resulting from this merging of the sexes in the workplace.

Now that it has become very clear that the emotional and romantic affairs of men and women on the job have everything to do with both performance and productivity, human resource people are becoming extremely interested in this potentially explosive situation. The emotions of the people who perform the tasks that bring us products and services not only affect productivity, but profoundly affect the bottom line as well. The business of men and women getting along on the job has become a major financial issue for corporations.

While Working America is catching its breath from its post-war evolution, it must now prepare solid answers for all the questions regarding men and women on the job that came up during the 1970s and 1980s. While women were thinking about how to get a good job with some growth opportunity—they neglected to anticipate what life would be like working shoulder-to-shoulder with men. Intent on getting inside the board rooms of America, women didn't anticipate fully what interpersonal relationships would be like once they took their seats. Now that women have definitely arrived and certainly plan on staying, many are concerned and confused as to how they should best deal with the possible and very likely complications of working closely with men.

And when women joined men in the workplace, they found that those men, who never had been offered much guidance, were used to playing by their own rules on the job and were confused as to what guidelines they were supposed to be following in the so-called new environment. Many of those men insisted that when women emerged on the workplace scene, they were just minding their own business and doing what they had always done to maintain their own identity while striving to exist in a highly competitive and tough business world.

So it really shouldn't be surprising to anyone that, now, with the door cracked open, the following situations are bursting out of the corporate closet:

- A Fortune 500 company offers professional counseling to a corporate couple—a male sales representative is dating a female systems engineer in the same office. Although the company does not have a policy forbidding coworkers to date, it is extremely sensitive to how such a relationship can affect the team dynamics of a division.

- A female bank officer is having an affair with her married and very high-level supervisor. He stays with his wife but the officer gets her promotions.

The other up-and-coming bank officer, a male, has been working day and night and feels he won't be going anywhere as long as the superior/subordinate affair continues to influence his boss's decision making. Lying awake at night, he analyzes his boss's affair with his coworker and realizes sadly that some other guy's sex life is affecting his ability to support his family.

- A large law firm creates a policy that no partners are allowed to date associates. Although it looks sound on paper, some partners have no intention of honoring the policy. They continue to carry on the personal and sometimes intimate relationships they have with one another. They feel the firm has no right to create lifestyle policies, and that personnel policies should not be personal policies.
- An attorney with the U.S. Securities and Exchange Commission in Washington, D.C, grew weary of women in her office having affairs with supervisors that led to promotions and raises. She sued, claiming that those affairs created an offensive and unfair work environment for the other women. The court agreed.

Meeting the Need

The need to improve the workplace climate for men and women on the job is immediate. It is obvious that I am not alone when I speak of the great urgency for a solid compilation of generally accepted rules. Because of the current surge of mixed messages to working people, including such statements as "men agree that work and sex do mix " and "you can find love and a husband on the job," there is even greater confusion about where the social and sexual lines are drawn, and where, when, and if those lines can be crossed safely during the workday.

All the human resource specialists and working people I spoke with agreed that it would make their jobs much easier if there were guidelines that led to a greater understanding among men and women and the companies for which they work. Because I believed that it was important that the information found within the pages of this book be widely accepted and followed, I sought out people who have spent a good deal of their working lives helping people be better professionals. I am especially appreciative of the assistance offered by the many individuals from IBM; Mr. Theodore E. Payne of Xerox; Mr. Tom Dailey of Sierra Research; Mr. Allan Seigel of Arent, Fox, Kintner, Plotkin & Kahn; General Jack Merritt, United States Army Retired; Dr. Jean A. Hamilton of the Institute for Research on Women's Health; Laura Loeb of the Congressional Caucus for Women's Issues; Bernice Sanders of the Project on the Status and Education of Women; and Claudia Withers of the Womens Legal Defense Fund.

The information within this book is most definitely *not* an attempt to criticize the behavior or actions of any particular individuals or companies, including those involved in my own personal experience with sexual harassment and all its complexities. But *Corporate Attractions* is intended to be a thoughtful attempt to begin bridging the broad gap between employees and employees, employers and employees, and business and the courts.

When I began to counsel other working people and listen to their problems, I knew that individuals needed some sort of access to good guidance, and there simply weren't enough resources available to provide counseling to all who needed help. The crying need was confirmed by

Barbara Gutek in her six-year academic study released in 1988 entitled "Sex and the Workplace." In her study, Ms. Gutek reveals that more than 80 percent of workers report some kind of social-sexual experience on the job and that as many as 35 million Americans have one such experience each week.

It is my hope that *Corporate Attractions* will be an important beginning to an essential effort for better everyday communication between those 35 million people and the companies that employ them. I also hope that it will help prevent employees and employers from landing in court. I offer my personal account of sexual harassment—and the events that surrounded and followed my experience—only as a case study for the reader to dissect, examine, study and finally draw necessary conclusions from—for within this account lie some very valuable lessons that *only* a true story can teach us.

PART ONE:

AN INSIDE ACCOUNT OF SEXUAL HARASSMENT

Chapter 1

Off with Her Head

"Let the jury consider their verdict," the King said.
"No, no!" said the Queen. "Sentence first-verdict afterwards."
"Stuff and nonsense!" said Alice loudly. "The idea of having the sentence first!"
"Hold your tongue!" said the Queen, turning purple.
"I won't!" said Alice.
"Off with her head!" the Queen shouted at the top of her voice. Nobody moved.

Alice's Adventures in Wonderland
Lewis Carroll

Friday afternoon, October 23, 1981

Everyone in the room was sitting perfectly still. There was a dead silence in the executive office of the general manager. I was seated on the edge of the sofa situated near the window, somewhat physically removed from the others in the room, nervously squeezing my fingers together. The three men sat stiff and motionless in their chairs around the desk of "Dino" Dinovitz, vice president and general manager of WGR-TV, Channel 2, a Buffalo, New York television station. My hands felt like ice. My heart was pounding and I was having considerable trouble breathing.

I had just told Dinovitz that my supervisor, Tom Cochran, had made serious sexual advances toward me and it wasn't something I was going to allow—and it was something I didn't think the station should allow, either. No one was going to tell me I had to perform sexual favors in order to advance my career. Surely the company would not condone this type of threat, let alone allow my boss to assault me physically. Not only did I have trouble accepting that such a terrible thing had happened to me at work, but I had just as much trouble talking about it. The morals I had tried to live my life by had never before been challenged in such a direct and confrontational way. In my wildest dreams, I never thought I would have to defend my own deepest principles to my employer. But now everything I believed in was suddenly on the line. All because my married boss decided he wanted to sleep with me. I found it nearly unbelievable and very frightening.

Dino finally spoke.

"Let me get this straight," he said in a careful and controlled tone of voice that indicated to me he didn't quite know what to do and was stalling for time until he could figure out what it was he was supposed to say.

"OK," he paused, "you say Tom sexually harassed you." He nodded in my direction with a look of both scorn and disbelief on his boyish face, "And you also say that you reported this, this 'harassment' to Jim."

With equal intensity he shifted his stare to Jim Conshafter who sat frozen and wooden before him. "Did she report this to you?" he asked Jim, the general sales manager, hoping he would get the answer he needed to hear, the answer the company needed to hear.

Jim's answer was barely audible. It was obvious he was too shaken to speak. Finally, he could only nod his head once or twice much as if he had a nervous twitch. His face was ashen, and for a moment, I felt sorry for him. I had always liked Jim. He had appeared to be a hardworking guy with his share of integrity, a family man, and someone I thought I could trust. Yes, I had reported the harassment to him—almost four months earlier. It had not been easy, but I had gone into Jim Conshafter's office and told him what was happening to me. Not only did I want his help in handling this terrifying situation, but I had to report the harassment to management, didn't I? It had said so in our company policy. My parents and friends had convinced me it was the right thing and I had believed it was the only thing to do. What my supervisor had asked for was against the law.

Dino was still struggling with what was before him. Although I was still frightened, my original indignation was returning. He obviously didn't know how to handle the situation, and that could only mean trouble for me.

I could tell he was grasping for a way to phrase his next question correctly. It was going to be an important one. Tom Cochran was a newly promoted manager. He was one of the first blacks to be promoted to a management position in the Taft Broadcasting organization. Channel 2 had not been particularly well known for offering solid management opportunities to minorities. Promoting Cochran from cameraman to account executive and now to local sales manager was one of the first significant affirmative action moves the company had made. As the first woman account executive in the history of the television station, I was the other.

"Did you harass Neville, Tom?"

More silence.

Finally Cochran answered Dino's pointed question the same non-verbal way Jim Conshafter had answered. But this time, the side-to-side motion of his head indicated no. No, he was saying, he hadn't harassed me.

"Well, then," said Dino, as though some conclusion had been reached. He motioned to me in his always evident Dale Carnegie style, "You say you were harassed by Tom yet Tom says that he did no such thing." He thought a minute and then went on, this time with a harder edge to his voice, "You know, if I were Tom and you had made such an accusation about me, I wouldn't want you to work for me, anymore." He seemed satisfied with his statement. He paused. It was coming. "I guess the best the thing for us to do is for you to find yourself another job. You have two weeks to do so." He had solved the problem. It was final. He wanted to be out of this uncomfortable situation. In fact, more than that, he needed to get out of his office and away from these two managers who evidently had messed up. And he definitely wanted to get away from this troublesome woman.

When we had surprised him at the beginning of our unscheduled meeting, Dino had said that he and his wife had dinner plans that evening and that he couldn't meet with us for long—he could only spare a few minutes. But that was before he knew what the meeting was all about. Now, instead of dinner with his wife, he needed to place a private telephone call to the corporate office and company attorneys in Cincinnati, Ohio, and make sure that he had handled the situation properly. He wanted no blemishes on his career at Taft, and a sexual harassment lawsuit coming from the Taft station he was managing might qualify as one. He was 31 and running a television station was new to him, let alone dealing with an explosive personnel problem. He didn't want any part of this.

My fear turned to anger. "I have no intention of leaving my job," I stated to all of them. "I do well here and I like my job. I will not go looking for another job, but I will look for a lawyer."

There, I had said it. Evidently the decision was made. Pushed to the wall, I was going to fight. The problem was, I had no idea how to fight something as ugly as this. And already things didn't look good. It was starting off as three against one.

I took a deep breath and my sometimes dormant but ever-present strong will kicked in like an emergency engine on a plane going down. With much more confidence than I felt, I said very calmly and even rather briskly, "It's fairly obvious you don't know how to handle this type of problem, Dino." My forced "knowing" air brought a look of rage to Dino's face, but I continued, "And I'm afraid nothing is going to be resolved this evening. I can assure you that over the weekend I will obtain a lawyer to represent me. And, in the presence of my lawyer, I would like to meet with you first thing Monday morning. And," I said finally, "I have *no* plans to leave this company."

My dress was now soaked with sweat. I was going to cry. I was never going to work again. My career in television was over. It was Friday night and I needed some tissues and a lawyer. I barely heard Dino's last remark asking me who I thought I was and who the hell was in charge around here, anyway? I got up as gracefully as I could and hoped that I walked out of the room in a dignified manner. Even as I left, I noticed that nobody moved.

As I drove out of the parking lot into the rainy night, no

longer bothering to hold back the tears, I was pretty sure the three managers I had left behind in Dino's office were figuring out how to dispose of my body, at least in a personnel sense. Dino had just as much said they had to get rid of me somehow. And there was no doubt in my own mind, that I would fight them all the way.

That was the beginning of what would be a seven-year battle. After thinking several months of being sexually harassed by my boss was a bad dream, I now sensed the real nightmare was yet to come.

Chapter 2

Golden Days

All in the golden afternoon
Full leisurely we glide;
For both our oars, with little skill,
By little arms are plied,

Alice's Adventures
in Wonderland
Lewis Carroll

March 1981

"She really has come into her own," read my 1981 yearly performance evaluation written by my supervisor, James Conshafter, then the local sales manager. She is most definitely management material. Kathleen is a good person with a fine future with Taft. Overall appraisal of this person: Outstanding."

It was my third year with WGR-TV, and I was happy with my supervisor's comment. My job with the television station was really working out well. I felt that I really had come into my own. Besides having what I thought was the honor and distinction of being the first woman account executive in the history of the Taft-owned station, I had found a position that offered me many opportunities to blend all of my professional interests. As an account executive, I was marketing a product I liked: the medium of television. As a part of that creative marketing process, I had many opportunities to write and produce television commercials. And, as if that weren't enough to term my job ideal, because of my previous experience in sales promotion and fashion for an area women's specialty store chain, I was also the on-air consumer reporter for the nationally syndicated program, "PM Magazine." Although I was only 27, my career seemed to be moving right along. Knowing how rare such an experience was, I felt fortunate to have a position that was creative, challenging, and well paid. So, having just been named Career Woman of the Year by the Business and Professional Women's Foundation, the phrase Jim Conshafter had used on my job evaluation about "having a bright future," looked as though it might be true.

Because I felt so fortunate to have found my career niche, I diligently began to organize and form a professional volunteer counseling group I called Women in Touch, or WIT. The group consisted of successful women representing a variety of fields from medicine to law to broadcasting. It was our job to answer questions and act as mentors to high school seniors who were interested in pursuing particular fields with which we were already familiar—our own. We gave the young women insight into the best colleges for their professions, leads on internships they should pursue, and, in general, offered ways to help them best prepare for their chosen careers.

As founder of the organization, I spent some of my evenings speaking to various audiences about the group's purpose and worthwhile efforts. Because I believed in what we were doing, if it was a little extra work for me, I really didn't notice. I believed in the program and wanted others to share my enthusiasm.

Since college I had always been closely involved and interested in the personal and professional development of young women. Since my own days of competing in the Miss America program, I had trained many young women for dance and scholarship competitions, given private instruction, and held various positions on the board of directors for America's Junior Miss—the largest scholarship program for women in the country. In fact, the television industry and the Junior Miss program have always had a lot in common as many former Junior Misses have gone on to become major television journalists and personalities. Diane Sawyer, first of CBS and now ABC, Mary Frann of "The Bob Newhart Show," Debra Norville of NBC News, and Kathie Lee Gifford of "LIVE: Regis and Kathie Lee" are all alumnae of the Junior Miss Scholarship Program (now known as Outstanding Young Woman of America.)

So Women in Touch fit naturally in with my other volunteer efforts. Because it was obviously such a needed program, it was very well received in the western New York State area by educators, human resource people, and women in general. Because of the overwhelming regional enthusiasm, I anticipated that it would not be long before it became a national program.

My third year with Channel 2 was certainly a fulfilling one. I enjoyed my job and I was getting the chance to see some of my own personal dreams come true.

So I was faced with a tough decision that spring when the number one station in the Buffalo market asked me to join them. There had been other job offers since I had come to Channel 2, but this was one opportunity I had to think hard about. After giving the offer much thought, I decided to accept it. Owned by Capital Cities, Inc., Channel 7 was a first-rate operation. Not only did the opportunity offer me a better position, but it allowed me to advance my career without leaving my hometown area. Being able to remain within close proximity to my family was an important consideration when it came to my employment plans. In the field of broadcasting, it's pretty rare that you are able to make a move within a market. It is more likely the case that you have no choice but to relocate in order to advance your career. Fortunately, at this point in my own career, I had been offered another option. But I never made it to Channel 7.

I had accepted the position at Channel 7 late Friday afternoon and planned to give my notice at Channel 2 on Monday morning. Because of the competitive nature of television, there is no such thing as a two-week notice when you are leaving to go work for another TV station. As soon as I gave notice, I would leave immediately.

But when I arrived at work on Monday morning, I found that giving notice was going to be a problem. My boss, Jim Conshafter, was home sick with the flu and wouldn't be coming in that day. Because I was expected at my new position by noon, I had no choice but to call Jim at home and let him know about my decision.

Jim seemed genuinely upset. He told me he would be right in and asked that I wait for him. While I was waiting, he apparently called the station manager, Dino Dinovitz, and told him about my intention to leave. It soon became obvious that Dino was going to help Jim convince me not to take the offer.

Dinovitz called me into his office and began to do his part to persuade me to stay. "You'll be making a big mistake," he said in a wise and knowing manner. "Your career is going well, but no one can afford to make even one judgment error in this business. One bad move and you lose your momentum. It's something you never get back."

I was listening intently. One thing I didn't want to do was make a mistake. I had thrown everything into my career and it was important to me. I certainly didn't want to make a wrong move.

"You are important to the Taft organization," he revealed. "We raised you. We trained you. Maybe you aren't aware of this, but we have you picked to become one of our next Taft managers. You can write your own ticket with this company. After all, people like you don't come along every day, especially a woman of your caliber."

This was the first time I had ever heard Dino even admit that women were part of the organization. When he first came to Channel 2 as general manager, I had taken note immediately in various meetings that he referred to female clients as "gals." I assumed that the females who worked for Channel 2 were also "gals." I had no idea he took female employees seriously, this was a revelation to me.

Having delivered his last remark, he beamed. He was pleased with the reaction he was seeing on my face. I anticipated it would be mildly uncomfortable giving my notice, but I surely didn't think management would be so intent on keeping me. And, I thought, I had been very happy at Channel 2. In fact, I loved my job. I began to reconsider.

Dino finally pulled out his ace. In a most sincere and gentle voice, he spoke to me as if he was revealing a trusted secret, "You are the most valuable employee on the team. We can't lose you," he stressed, "especially not to our competitors."

He laid it on pretty thick, making me uncomfortable.

The comment about losing me to one of the competitors stuck in my mind.

The morning wore on and, between Jim and Dino I got the complete treatment. Dino told me he would do no other work that day so that he could be available to me. Conshafter was sick but refused to go home until I told him I would stay. Finally, I called the sales manager of Channel 7 and told him I wouldn't be accepting the position, after all. He was furious. Apparently the station had planned a warm welcome for me. Now that I wasn't showing, they felt foolish, and, admittedly, so did I. Without question, I had burned a bridge. There would never be another offer from Channel 7. I hoped I had done the right thing.

The next day, Dino reassured me in a note that I had made the right decision and that I would never regret it. In his note, he also thanked me for my loyalty. I was glad that he had mentioned loyalty because that was one of the two reasons I had decided to stay. The other reason was that he and Conshafter had firmly convinced me that staying with Taft would offer me a fairly certain opportunity to move up quickly into a management position. At Channel 7, I had no real guarantee that promotions would happen as quickly.

Within a few weeks after I had received and turned down the offer from Channel 7, Jim Conshafter was promoted to the number two position at the station, general sales manager. With the position of local sales manager left open, a few days later one of my fellow members of the department, Sylvester Thomas Cochran filled the available management slot thereby becoming my new boss.

Chapter 3

The Trap

There were doors all round the hall, but they were all locked; and when Alice had been all the way down one side and up the other, trying every door, she walked sadly down the middle, wondering how she was ever going to get out again.

Alice's Adventures in Wonderland
Lewis Carroll

Excerpts from 1981 journal

First entry, undated:

Even though I knew better, I was still impatient. I had been waiting almost an hour for an available soundbooth. Just prior to the airing of the six o'clock newscast was a bad time to expect to find any soundbooth that wasn't already in use by someone editing last minute news segments.

I was anxious to hear the audio tape I held in my hand. Earlier today, the production manager of the station had given me a track of a musical score that had been written "on spec" as part of an advertising campaign designed to promote the image of a local bank. He had asked me to listen to the tape and come up with lyrics that could be adapted to the musical score. I always leaped at the chance to write lyrics, and today was no exception.

At last, a young editor came scrambling out one of the booths, balancing a pile of tapes in his arms. As I watched him make his noisy exit through the studio door, I took his place in the booth, relieved that the news broadcast had begun. At least I would be able to work for the next half-hour without any interruptions. It was always like a tomb in the back of the production area while the news was being broadcast. I would have total peace and quiet.

I pushed the tape in and began to listen intently. I liked it. Unlike many jingles its distinct melody was strongly mixed with the sound of strings. It was a good piece of music. Writing lyrics to such a score shouldn't take me long, I thought. Already, I had an idea for the refrain.

The arms around my waist came from nowhere. I felt his hands tighten around me as they began to move. I gripped the cassette deck in front of me and held my breath. I stared straight ahead. I couldn't turn around. I'd be face-to-face with him. I was trapped.

Slowly and carefully, I asked Cochran what he wanted.

Several seconds seemed to pass as I felt and listened to his breath on the back of my neck. My stomach was sick.

"It must be the dress you have on today," he finally whispered in my ear.

Still I didn't move.

After a few more minutes, he left as quietly as he came. I shuddered. I could still feel exactly where his hands had been. It was then that I noticed the tape had long since finished playing. I slowly pulled it out. The words to the song were gone.

(Gave my black and white dress to my mother—she cannot understand why I don't want it. I told her I don't like the way it fits. I'm going to try to forget the incident in the soundbooth ever happened.)

Late May:

As I pulled out of the station a little before 6 p.m. on a Friday, I suddenly remembered I had to stop first at the dry cleaner before going on to meet Mary Hutchinson and her fiancé at Lord Chumley's. If I hurried, I wouldn't be late.

Mary was a media buyer for a local advertising agency and totally unlike any other media buyer I had met through my work at WGR-TV. Not only was she witty, but she also possessed an uncanny ability to size people up properly. She knew people as well as she knew numbers. In fact, she probably knew them even better.

I parked in front of the dry cleaner and quickly glanced in my rearview mirror before opening my car door into the passing traffic. I suddenly stopped. Cochran was in his car, right behind me. Instead of getting out of my car, I kept my head down and fiddled with the dials on the radio. Maybe he hadn't follow me here, I reasoned. Maybe he just had drycleaning to pick up, too and in a minute would be gone.

He was at my car window.

"Where are you going?" he asked as I reluctantly rolled down the window.

I hesitated. I didn't feel comfortable lying to him. After all, he was my new boss, and, in fact, had only been my boss for a little over a month.

"Well, actually, Mary Hutchinson and I are meeting for dinner at Lord Chumley's, and if I don't hurry I'm going to be late." I said as I quickly got out of my car, forcing him to move aside. "Have a nice weekend," I murmured over my shoulder as I stepped inside the door of the dry cleaner. I noticed that he apparently didn't need to make a stop there, after all.

I immediately spotted Mary and Steve at the bar. She motioned me to come over as I edged my way through the after-work crowd. After telling me that we would have a table in a few minutes, Mary instantly launched into one of her humorous stories about something that had happened that day at work. If she hadn't, I might have told her I was beginning to feel some uneasiness regarding my boss's behavior toward me. But even if she hadn't already been busily engaged in telling an antecdote, I'm not sure I would have known what to tell her. And besides, it would have been slightly awkward. Although she was a friend, she was also a client.

Mary stopped midway through an animated sentence. "Hey, what's Cochran doing here?" she demanded, wide-eyed, as she stared toward the door.

Without asking if he could, he joined us. After mumbling hello to Steve, he sat quietly with the three of us while Mary continued on with her story. I ignored him. He had one drink and left

When he had gone, Mary carefully commented, "How odd. Don't you think it's rather odd that he showed up here? I wouldn't think Lord Chumley's is his kind of place," she speculated softly. She was silent and looked thoughtful.

"Yes," she spoke firmly, "it is really odd that he showed up, didn't have anything to say, and then just took off." She ended the discussion about his brief and strange appearance with one final question, which she directed at me. "I just wonder what it was he wanted?"

I didn't answer but, unfortunately, I thought I knew.

June 11

I spoke this weekend at the New York State Business and Professional Women's Foundation annual conference in the Catskills Mountains. I love that part of the state—it was a pretty drive down and back. I've been so busy lately, it was good to get away, even if it was for a conference. Big crowd. Met many women who were interested in helping with the Women in Touch program. I'm very encouraged about the program's future.

June 12

Cochran was really bugging me today about going to Rochester to see the media director of Manufacturer's Hanover Bank. He keeps insisting we need to talk to her about the winter hockey buy, but he and I both know it is premature to schedule a meeting. He's acting very strange. I really don't have time this week to lose a day being out of town.

June 15

I thought we would never arrive at the station. Although Rochester, New York, is less than two hours from Buffalo, the trip back with my boss seemed endless. As soon as his car came to a safe halt, I was going to jump—no, I was going to leap out—and run into the station. And I was more than ready to make my fast exit—I had my client file in one hand and my other hand on the door. We just needed to get there.

I knew my instincts had been right when I had thought Cochran had other motives for insisting that he accompany me to see a client in Rochester. Even the client couldn't figure out why he was so persistent about seeing her, when, in fact, it was months before her contract needed to be renegotiated.

But if she had been curious as to his motives for going with me to Rochester, so was I. It wasn't until after the client meeting, when I was alone in Cochran's car with him—and after he had grabbed me and kissed me square on the mouth—and told me all the things he said he had been wanting to tell me—that I knew the real and disgusting reason why we had made the trip.

After I had pulled myself away and told him, in very clear terms, that he had no right *ever* to touch me, I realized he wasn't comprehending what I was telling him. In fact, I was sure he couldn't even hear the disgust and horror I felt for his actions that rang in my every word to him.

During the drive back to Buffalo, he proceeded to upset me more by telling me all about his fantasy-like rationalizations as to why "he had to do it." He wondered what it would be like for us to lie together. I tried not to listen. I thought, instead, of what I wanted my four brothers to do to him. I concentrated on blocking him out. I had a couple of hours before I could get out of that car so I had to stay in control. I moved as close to the passenger door as I could and continued to stare out the window at nothing.

But his monologue continued. He even seemed boastful about the fact that he had "wanted to do that for a long time." He seemed totally and completely oblivious to the fact that he had violated me physically and continued to do so emotionally by forcing me to listen to his intimate thoughts about me.

The simple and unvaried architecture of Channel 2 never looked so good to me as we pulled into the parking lot earlier this afternoon. As Cochran put the car into park, and as I was about to begin my well-planned dash out of his Buick, he stopped me dead in my tracks. But so did the foreboding and threatening message he left me with. "You do everything right," he said gravely, "And you will go a long way with this company." He looked to me , expecting an answer. "It's all up to you."

Instead of running, I walked slowly into the station. I didn't need to hurry anymore. My career had just come to a screeching halt.

June 15, later

After getting out of the car, rather than going to my own office I went upstairs to the lunchroom. There was a telephone there, and I was able to call my friend, Joanie, without fear of Cochran walking into my office. Joan is a buyer at the store chain I used to work for; and she and her twin sister Joyce are two of my closest friends. I trust them. I could tell either of them anything. But I became upset today, when I tried to tell Joan what had happened. Her response told me I was not overreacting. "Oh God, Kath," she had gasped. "This is terrible. You can't work for him. If I were you I'd be afraid of him from now on. He could do anything." She added, "It turns my stomach that he touched you. Broad daylight—what a slime. Leave work, right now," she had commanded. "It's almost five, anyway—just leave, Kath. Get out of there—we'll talk later."

As soon as I got off the phone with Joanie, I left my office. I went straight to my apartment and took a shower. I had thought it might help wash away the fact that my boss had his hands on me. And my mouth, I had thought, as I washed my face with a vigorous vengeance. No one touches me who I don't want touching me. I couldn't believe he was trying to make some sort of sick deal with me. I'd have to quit my job, I guessed. People wouldn't understand why I walked out on a good job, but I didn't know how I could stay. My parents would understand. I would tell them the reason why I couldn't work there. I thought for a second about the man I had been seeing occasionally. I wondered what he would think—but I decided then and there I wouldn't tell him. The relationship was too new and this was too unpleasant. Besides, he was so consumed with his own career.

But if I did leave this job, I wouldn't be able to work in television locally, because after turning down the offer from Channel 7 there remained no other options. I'd have to get into something else. But that wasn't what I wanted.

What a jerk, he gets promoted and evidently thinks he can use his power to force the only woman on his staff to fool around with him. Evidently he is so stupid he thinks I'm part of his new fringe benefit package. What kind of man would threaten a woman—or anyone—who worked for him? Although he had been a coworker for more than two years, it had never occurred to me before, but Joanie was right today, when she said he was a slimy guy. And now it was my tough luck to have my career in his hands.

It would take more than a shower to make this problem go away.

June 16

Although he was not exactly optimistic about my future with the company, after talking to Tommy Brydges last night, I feel a little better. I saw him as I was headed to a fundraiser for Sheila Murphy, a former anchorwoman at Channel 2 who was now running for a spot on the city's common council. Tom's very level-headed and a smart attorney. I know he's right, I'll have to report it. I absolutely dread the thought of reporting this to Conshafter. Maybe I'll wait a few days. Cochran did not speak to me,today, nor did I speak to him. I loathe him for the position he has put me in.

June 20

I went in and out of Conshafter's office three times today before I was able to blurt out what had happened to me. I knew I couldn't procrastinate anymore because the annual Taft meeting is coming up this weekend and both Cochran and I will be there. I couldn't attend unless I thought Conshafter would straighten Cochran's act out before the conference. I like Jim Conshafter a lot but I was surprised at his reaction today. I had been so embarrassed to tell him about what Tom had done—and said—to me. After I had struggled with my story, and asked him what should be done—I had been horrified when Jim didn't say anything. He had just sat there behind his desk—appearing dumbfounded. Minutes had gone by and he still didn't say anything! Finally, he told me that he just didn't know what to say. That was it—he just didn't know what to say! Then, twice again, he said he didn't know what to say. I kept waiting for him to say something more but he never did. At last, awkwardly, I got up and thanked him for his time.

What a mess this is. I hope Jim will think about this and come up with a good way to handle it. I'm counting on him to pull Cochran aside and tell him to leave me alone.

Jim will do it—he's decent—he'll talk to Cochran. I just hope he does it before the Toronto meeting.

July 1

The Toronto meeting was a nightmare. Evidently Conshafter didn't talk to Cochran. Although I was there to receive an award, and the three-day event was supposed to be the company's best effort at stroking its employees, the entire trip seemed like a lifetime. Fortunately for me, I was assigned to share a room with one of the few other female employees in the television division—Andrea Brookman from Philadelphia. I didn't need to warn her that I was having a problem with Cochran—at the opening night cocktail party she immediately spotted it.

Cochran had been hovering around Andrea and me and finally chose to wrap his arm around me while Andrea and I continued to talk. I was shocked that he would publicly put his hands on me. There were many members of top management present, not to mention the fact that the president of Taft was involved in a conversation taking place on the other side of the room.

It seemed like forever when Cochran finally released his hold on my shoulder and decided to move away.

"Wow—what is it with that guy?" Andrea asked. "That guy is my boss." I told her.

The next morning Andrea and I headed for the health and fitness center at the hotel. "How can you work with that guy mauling you all the time" she asked me as she got off the stationary bike. I had only known Andrea a day, but I told her everything that had happened, including the fact that I had reported it to Conshafter.

"I'm sure I don't need to tell you this—but everything he is doing is serious. It's good you reported it. For the remainder of this trip, I'll stay close by you and make sure he keeps his distance. I can't believe he is a manager and actually thinks he can get away with this sort of thing. You would think we are beyond this."

Andrea was a great help to me, but there were a couple of moments when I was on my own. One night I had to go out to dinner with the staff from Buffalo. Because I heard what restaurant we were going to, I asked Andrea if she could arrange for her group from Philadelphia to have dinner at the same restaurant. Naturally, Cochran sat next to me and pressed his leg up against mine during the entire dinner. I was between the corner of the restaurant wall and him. As soon as dinner was over, I excused myself and asked Andrea if I could ride back to the hotel with her and the men she worked with. As we got out of the car at the hotel, one of the men quietly said to me that he guessed I had a problem on my hands and that he was really sorry about it. I wished this stranger was a coworker in Buffalo.

When Cochran called the room it was always Andrea who answered the phone. Thanks to Andrea—it was two against one when it came to forcing Cochran to keep his distance.

I was relieved when the final awards dinner was over and I could go back to my room. Andrea had just gone up in the elevator ahead of me, but I had been talking to one of the women employees from Virginia. Out of the blue, Cochran was at my side, again uttering something about taking me to the hotel disco and having some fun. He seemed totally oblivious to the fact that I wanted nothing to do with him.

I breathed a sigh of relief when I was finally on the elevator; this was wearing me out. When I got to the room, Andrea was still awake . "From the look on your face," she said, "I guess he found you. Apparently I can't leave you alone for a minute."

August

I'm really mad at Conshafter. Nothing has changed except for the fact that I had to beg the maintenance engineer to have someone reposition my desk. Cochran had the terrible habit of sneaking up behind me while I was on the phone and leaning against my back. My pen would fly up in the air whenever it happened. I felt like I was really taking some action by moving my desk but it hasn't done much good—not really.

September

I have explained to the secretary that I am working on a lot of fall programming availabilities and have found that the conference room is a good place to work without interruptions. I have not told her that I prefer the conference room because the door has a lock on it.

I don't go into work before 8:30 a.m. any more unless I have production work. I miss those early morning "head starts". Cochran started coming in earlier and there is no way I will be there alone—with him. Some days when I pull into the station and see only Cochran's car I drive around the block until one of the other members of our department arrives. It's a pain to do that but it makes things easier for me.

Late September

I took a day off to go to Washington, D.C., to work on gathering some interest there for the Women in Touch program. A local congressman, John LaFalce, and his staff had offered me a good deal of encouragement and support regarding my program. They had helped set up some of my informational meetings. I hoped that I had sounded committed to the program; I was concerned that I had not. I was tired and not feeling very well when I made the trip to Washington. It wasn't that I had lost my enthusiasm for the program, but I had lost the last thread of hope that Conshafter was going to help me. It has been over three months since I reported my problem to Jim. He hasn't said one word to me about it since that day in his office. I thought at least he would ask me how I was doing—or even ask if everything was all right. Anything—something.

I'm thinking about reporting it, again. In the past few months, I've realized that I can't give up my job and just walk away. I worked hard and was a good employee. It isn't fair that I would have to give up my job. Maybe things will change.

October

I can't take it anymore. I have the worst cold of my life. Tonight, I was the guest speaker at the Enchanted Mountains Business and Professional Women's Club and felt like a fraud. I had quoted the words of Pearl Buck—"a woman must be true to her deepest principles" as I began my speech about women advancing in business, and I felt disgusted with myself that I wasn't managing my own life and heeding those very words. During the drive back from Olean tonight I decided that I'm going to put a stop to this nonsense at work. Why had I let it go this long?

Chapter 4

Good-bye Golden Girl

There was a dead silence instantly, and Alice thought to herself, "I wonder what they will do next!"

Alice's Adventures in Wonderland
Lewis Carroll

October 1981

My boss was becoming increasingly hostile, and I was growing more exhausted by the day. But, oddly enough, his recent hostility had almost come as a welcome relief to me. I much preferred it to his previous and continual blatant harassment. With his hostility, however, came a new problem. It signaled to me that the game of harassment was almost over, and it looked like I was going to be the loser.

It had been more than four months since he had told me what the "sexual terms" of my job were, and although outwardly I wasn't allowing myself to appear rattled, I was starting to crumble on the inside. I had tried very hard over the past few months to protect my position at the station, but it was obvious there was nothing I could do. I was caught in a power crunch. If he wanted me out, he could do it. By now, it was very clear to him that I would not accede to his demands. I felt my failure to submit to his "other" job terms left him with only one option. He had to fire me. Frankly, I didn't know how he was going to do it—or when he was going to do it—but I guessed that it would probably be soon. He had no choice, I thought, and, for that matter, neither did Conshafter.

As things turned out, I didn't have to wait long to find out how—and when—my boss would fire me.

On Monday morning, October 19, the meteorologist from the newsroom called and asked me if I needed a ride to the "Get High On Yourself" anti-drug luncheon scheduled for that day. I was glad he had called because I hadn't put any details down on my calendar and I needed to be filled in on the particulars of the event. He told me that the students at my former high school—Wilson—had joined the NBC-sponsored, Paul Newman-inspired crusade on drug abuse awareness and were staging a press conference featuring local celebrities who supported the program. The event was intended to generate a great deal of publicity for both the cause and the kids from Wilson who had been the first students in the region to take such an initiative.

It had been ten years since my graduation from Wilson, and this was not my first visit since then. My first "official" return visit to my old school had been just months before.

In May the board of education, faculty, and students of Wilson High School had surprised me by staging a "Kathleen Neville Day." I was deeply touched and extremely honored that on the ten-year anniversary of my graduation from high school, they had chosen me as an outstanding graduate of my class. On the day they had designated, I had addressed the students at an assembly and afterwards had attended a reception held in the school's library, where my former teachers, family, and friends were in attendance. I was really more than a little embarrassed at the lengths they had gone to make me feel like a heroine. I couldn't help but wonder what they would think of me now if they knew their honoree had a sexual harassment problem with her boss and didn't know how to handle it.

During the reception, one of my former teachers proudly led me along the walls of the library to show me the "highlights of my life" exhibit the faculty had constructed. Adorning the walls were specially mounted pictures and clippings of my days as a student and later shots of me during my life in the working world. It was like a walking scrapbook and looked much more impressive than my own pile of jammed together photos and clippings that I had somewhere at home. They even included all sorts of photographs from my performances in the Miss Rochester and Miss New York programs. I was overwhelmed. Obviously, someone had gone to a lot of trouble to put the exhibit together.

Aside from the fact that I really believed the "Get High on Yourself" program was important, I particularly wanted to honor my invitation to the event because it had been issued by my own high school. Wilson High School had personally and very recently done so much for me; I wanted to return the support.

The meteorologist proceeded to tell me that we needed to be there by 12:30 p.m. and that two other Channel 2 staffers had also been invited and were attending. Ted Darling, the voice of the Buffalo Sabres, and Stan Coleman, the features reporter, would also be going to the event. For the sake of convenience, we decided that we would all ride together in the newscruiser. Because we were the NBC affiliate and—by no coincidence—NBC was the national sponsor, the newsroom was going to do a special feature on the event that would air that evening during the 5:30, 6:00, and 11:00 p.m. newscasts.

As it turned out, because of another news story that delayed the cameraman, we were late starting out for the event. But, neither the students nor the teachers seemed to notice or mind that we weren't there on time. They were just delighted that so many public officials and community leaders had supported and were attending their carefully planned activity. They had a terrific showing and the program was a tremendous success. I was proud that my high school alma mater had taken on such an ambitious project and that it had been such a hit.

We returned to the television station shortly after 2 p.m. My department was deserted; the only other person around was the sales secretary. Out of casual curiosity, I asked her where everyone else was—things seemed strangely quiet. The secretary said she thought most of the men were at the Quarterback Club.

I didn't know much about the Quarterback Club other than that it was a Monday noontime event following a Buffalo Bills home game and the men in my department looked forward to attending it. Although I was a Bills fan, it never really bothered me that they hadn't asked me to join them.

Everyone started straggling back in around 2:30 p.m. At that time, Cochran mentioned that there would be a department meeting at 5:30 p.m. I wasn't very happy at the thought of an end-of-the-day meeting. I had been at work since before 6 a.m. because of some last-minute details that needed to be done on a series of commercials. It was going to be a long day.

All of us were in Cochran's office at 5:30. Just before the meeting was about to start, I casually suggested that everyone look at the television monitor in Cochran's office that was tuned to Channel 2. Although the volume was down, the 5:30 p.m news was on and the screen was showing the shots taken at the "Get High on Yourself" press conference I had attended earlier that day. It was a nice feature and for the few minutes it was running, I mentioned to my coworkers about some of the highlights of the conference.

The next day, Cochran called me into his office and asked me to shut the door. He then proceeded to ask me why I hadn't told him where I had gone the previous day. For several minutes I remained puzzled. I couldn't figure out what he was getting at—but I knew he was aiming at something. "The luncheon," he said coldly, "Why didn't you tell me you were going to the luncheon?" He went on to tell me that I was to inform him of my whereabouts at all times and that I had not gotten his permission to go to the luncheon. In fact, I was not allowed to go anywhere during the day without his knowing where I was at all times.

I couldn't think of anything to say. What he was saying had me speechless. He must be talking about the Wilson High event, I thought. But, he couldn't mean that. I did that on behalf of Channel 2—NBC, our network, had sponsored that program. In fact, he wasn't even around when I went to it. That was the same day he and the other members of the department were at the Buffalo Bills luncheon. It was absurd.

In my mind the red light was definitely blinking. The time had arrived. He was setting me up to fire me. I got up. "When is Jim Conshafter due back?" I asked evenly. Jim was in Chicago on business.

Cochran didn't answer me. Instead he just stared.

I asked him again, "When will Jim be back?" My voice was just as firm as his stare.

"Friday. Jim will be back on Friday." He was spitting the words out as though he wanted to hit me with them. He didn't seem to like my question.

"I need to meet with you and Jim when he gets back." I emphasized Jim's name. "In fact on this matter, I don't think I could feel comfortable meeting alone with you."

As far as I was concerned, enough was enough. I was upset with both Conshafter and Cochran. But most of all, I was angry with myself. Things should never have gotten to this point. The only thing I could do now was start to take some control over a situation that had been out of control far too long.

Later that day, Cochran left a note on my desk telling me that he had spoken to Conshafter by telephone and our meeting with him was scheduled for Friday at 4 p.m. I wondered what else they had talked about on the phone. I decided I needed some help.

I called Tom Brydges, a lawyer and a friend, and asked him if I could have lunch with him. I told him I needed to talk to him right away and he agreed to see me the next day.

Tom was already familiar with most of my story. He had heard the initial facts in June, when Cochran first started harassing me. At that time, I had chosen Tom Brydges to confide in regarding what was happening to me at work. He was the right person to talk to about such a sensitive matter. Besides being a friend, he was an excellent labor attorney, who represented major corporations in all different types of labor matters. He would understand why I was concerned.

I had known Tom and his family for years; many people did. His late father had been a highly celebrated New York State senator who had done great things for the area. In fact, years before I was born, my own grandfather, as majority leader of the governing board of the county, had been one of the first politicians to endorse Tom's father for state senator. The Brydges family had grown up in the same little town of Wilson in which my four brothers and I had been raised. I trusted him completely.

Tom Brydges listened quietly to the latest developments with my boss. I told him that within one week's time, I had been criticized twice by Cochran for incidents that he or anyone else at Channel 2 normally wouldn't consider deserving of a reprimand. I probably bored Tom a little when I began to cite major errors others in the department had been responsible for since I had been with Channel 2, but I needed him to know how unusual these recent criticisms were in my business. Normally, whenever an account executive had a problem with a client, instead of criticizing the account executive Cochran or Conshafter always pitched in to help correct the error or mistake. Errors are very common in the television business, I told Tom, because so many different people and departments are involved in the placement and airing of commercials. Sometimes no one would even be sure who was really responsible for an error. On many occasions both Cochran and Conshafter had laughed about their own disastrous errors. I couldn't believe they would now try to use such a flimsy excuse as my involvement in community activities and even go as far as searching for errors—before they might happen—to make it look as though I was falling down on the job or was incompetent. I had never once been reprimanded by anyone at Channel 2 regarding my performance, I told Tom. I was positive I was being set up and I was beginning to feel frantic.

He put down his sandwich and sighed. "You're probably going to get fired," he said slowly and rather sadly. "I'm awfully sorry it's turning out this way for you." He shook his head. "I was afraid this would happen. In fact, I told you back in June that I suspected they would handle things this way."

I didn't respond. I looked down at my salad and didn't feel like eating anymore. My stomach was in a knot. I hadn't done anything wrong. Why did I have lose my job? I didn't want to face what was going to happen.

Tom continued. "I know it's a hard thing to accept and it doesn't seem fair—because, in fact, it really isn't fair. But if it's any consolation—you did the right thing—and that's important. You reported him. Not everyone is willing to do that. All you can do now is keep on doing the right thing. And, please let me know how your meeting on Friday turns out. And, Kath, I hope I'm wrong about this."

I hoped he was, too.

The tension during the next few days was unbearable. Cochran left a note on my desk that one of my client's spots was about to air incorrectly, but that he had managed to fix it before it happened. He was obviously searching hard for mistakes in my work. Even though the clerical error he had found was quite minor, it upset me that he had found even one.

On Friday morning, Conshafter passed me in the hall and barely spoke to me. If his demeanor was any indication, the meeting at 4 p.m. was going to be difficult. Although I was apprehensive, I was relieved that things were finally going to be out on the table. I just hoped I could live with the outcome.

To reassure myself, I looked into the folder I had prepared for the 4 p.m. meeting. As Tom Brydges had instructed me to do back in June, I had documented the incidents of sexual harassment, including the date and time when I had first reported the harassment to Conshafter. I also had my own copy of the company's policy prohibiting sexual harassment. I desperately hoped it was more than a piece of paper to Jim Conshafter, and that he even knew it existed.

I went into Conshafter's office promptly at four. Instead of saying hello, he ignored me and picked up the phone to tell Cochran to come in. A sullen Cochran came in and pulled up a chair next to Conshafter. Together, they were both staring at me.

"What did you need this meeting for?" asked Jim. He wasn't staring, after all, I thought. He was glaring at me, and I was already nervous enough.

I started to speak and then stopped. I didn't know how to start. I tried again, realizing that I had to get my feelings across to both of these men. It was now or never. Although my voice was a little shaky, I went straight to my point.

"A couple of months ago, you began—and continued—to sexually harass me. I told you to leave me alone—but you didn't." I raised my chin as I looked at Cochran. I decided I wasn't nervous anymore, I was furious. Cochran had a serious problem and unfortunately his problem had become mine. And now, once again, whether he liked it or not, it was going to become Conshafter's, too.

I looked at Conshafter. Although now slightly softer, my voice clearly showed my disappointment in him. "You already know all about this, Jim. I reported it to you—right in the beginning. But as far as I know, you did nothing to help me. And now, I feel as though I have no choice but to bring up this matter, again." I paused for a moment, "I have the company's policy regarding sexual harassment right here in front of me. It says that it isn't allowed in this company."

I took the policy from the folder resting on my lap and held it out to both of them. I was not surprised that neither Conshafter nor Cochran acknowledged my gesture.

Neither of them said anything, but I could tell they both seemed to have their own thoughts about what I had just said. In fact, so did I. And at that moment, it occurred to me that I blamed Conshafter more than I did Cochran.

Jim looked as though he was going to fall over. He fumbled with his phone, and it bounced on his desk before he managed to finally bring it to his ear.

"Dino. Dino," he stammered, "I, uh—well, actually we need to see you. Neville and Cochran are in my office. We have a problem here, and..." He stopped. Dino was interrrupting him on the other end. "I know, I know, but it's important," he stressed. How ironic. Now, Jim Conshafter finally realized that what had happened to me was important.

Within minutes, we were all in Dino's office and that was when Dino told me to leave the company, and that I had two weeks to find another job. It was also at that meeting that I told him I had no intention of leaving the company, that I would see him on Monday morning, accompanied by my lawyer. Dino didn't know at the time that I really didn't have a lawyer.

Finding a lawyer over a weekend can be a problem. Tom Brydges was with his law partners somewhere up in Canada—in a cabin for the weekend—and couldn't be reached by telephone. I was at a complete loss as to who I could get to represent me on this matter. I didn't know whether there were lawyers in Buffalo who specialized in this type of discrimination, and if there were, I really didn't have much time to find one. I had never needed a lawyer before now. My own words, from one of my segments on PM Magazine, suddenly came back to haunt me. Earlier that year, I had devoted one segment to advising people about the importance of having readily available access to good legal advice before they find themselves in a legal jam. I stressed at the end of the segment, "Don't wait until you need a lawyer before you get one." It was great advice, I thought wryly. Too bad I hadn't followed it.

On the basis of a friend's recommendation, I called a Buffalo attorney who had done some legal work in the broadcasting field. He was unavailable, but I was able to get hold of his partner. He listened to the story I was already getting tired of telling, and told me to go to the meeting with Dino, and then call him afterward. But after talking to my father over the weekend, he advised me against dealing with the station management alone. Things had become too serious at that point, my father said. I needed to step back and let an attorney handle the matter.

I met my new attorney, Joe, at 8 a.m. Monday morning. His offices were located just two blocks from the television station. We were going to discuss my problem and then walk together to the station at 9.

I explained to Joe that I wanted him to help me work things out with the management of Channel 2. I also explained to him that I knew I needed third-party assistance when I realized on Friday that Conshafter was not going to help me. He had taken the path of least resistance, and he was going to go along with whatever Dino wanted. I thought Conshafter was afraid he would lose his job and it had become obvious to me that he would do anything to keep it. That's where Jim Conshafter and I differed.

How quickly it had become a David-and-Goliath battle, I told Joe. I needed some good legal help. It was the three top managers of the station against me.

But, regardless of the current situation, I told Joe that I hoped something could be resolved. I mentioned that until this situation with Cochran had arisen, I had had a good relationship with the Taft management in Cincinnati. In fact, I had recently received a personal note from Dudley Taft, president of Taft, praising my efforts as an employee and that he specifically praised my involvement in the community. I felt as though my relationship with Taft management, other than the problem I had experienced with Cochran, was a good one.

At 8:50 a.m., while I was still in his office, Joe called Dino to let him know that he would be accompanying me to the 9 a.m. meeting. Dino would not take his call. On Joe's advice, I called Dino right back and got through to him. He was emphatic. He would not meet with any lawyers. I told him I understood and that I would be over to meet with him alone. I immediately left Joe's office and headed down the street to the station, dreading the thought of meeting with Dino.

I arrived at the station a few minutes after 9. I went straight to Dino's office, but his secretary nervously told me he was in conference and unavailable. I wasn't sure what to do next so I went to my office, hoping that I somehow could manage to do some work. I would have given anything for a normal workday.

Propped up on my desk, was an official-looking letter marked personal and confidential. It was addressed to me and read:

Date: October 26, 1981

From: Tom Cochran

To: Kathleen Neville

Copies to: Mr. Paul Dinovitz
Mr. Jim Conshafter
Mrs. Sue Pearce

Subject:

This is to inform you, in writing, of your unexcused absence on Monday, October 26, 1981.

We were not notified of your absence either by phone nor notified in writing. I find this to be unexceptable [sic] and this tardiness adds to your already poor job performance.

Tom Cochran

Apparently it hadn't mattered that I had called Dino earlier that morning to tell him where I was and that I was on my way to the station. I looked at my watch and noticed that it was only 9:10 a.m. The letter was outrageous. Someone obviously had told Cochran to write such a letter. Whoever that someone was, I thought sarcastically, **he** also should have told him how to spell "unacceptable."

By 9:30 a.m., another letter marked personal and confidential was delivered to me by Dino's secretary. I was certainly getting a lot of mail:

October 26, 1981

From: Dino Dinovitz

To: Kathleen Neville
Tom Cochran

Copies to: Sue Pearce
Jim Conshafter
Frank Stewart

Dear Kathleen:

Sue Pearce has been invited to serve as an impartial investigator with respect to the claims made by Kathy Neville against Tom Cochran. Sue will conduct an exhaustive investigation to determine the charges filed on Friday afternoon.

There will be no restrictions in terms of who Sue may speak with and will have access to all files to conduct a full investigation.

Upon the completion of Sue's investigation, she will submit to me in writing her evalution of these circumstances.

Sincerely

Dino Dinovitz
Vice President and General Manager

My heart sank when I read the part about Sue Pearce, an accountant for the station, being chosen the so-called "impartial" investigator. She was the wrong person for the job but I knew immediately why she had been chosen. She was a woman and she was extremely loyal to Dino. But I couldn't imagine her being capable of being impartial, let alone being skilled enough to conduct an investigation.

I also noticed on the memo from Dino that the name Frank Stewart had been added. Evidently he was the Taft attorney from Cincinnati who was coaching Dino. Although Dino told me my attorney could not be involved at that point, apparently the company's attorney could. The investigation would not be a real one, I thought. They were just going through the motions.

Within minutes I received a call from Sue Pearce. She asked that I meet with her at 2:30 p.m.

At noon, I went to my lawyer's office, and showed him my mail and told him about the meeting with Sue Pearce. He said that he would accompany me to the meeting.

At 2:30, Joe arrived at the station but was stopped by Dino who asked him to leave the building. Having no other choice, Joe left, but he told me to cooperate fully with the investigation.

I went into Pearce's office alone. She was standing at the door with her arms folded. I couldn't imagine why, but for some strange reason she acted as though she found all of this "sexual harassment business" exciting. She obviously liked the fact that she had been included in this internal drama.

Pearce told me to be seated and took her place behind her desk. She carefully rearranged the papers in front of her. Finally, she cleared her throat. "Now," she said as though she were the chief disiplinarian at a strict girls' school, "as we understand it," she was reading off of a piece of paper, "you have raised certain allegations. I will be asking you a series of questions and I want you to answer them for me. Do you understand what I have just said?" She stopped reading and looked up. I looked at her closely. Her lips were pursed and she was waiting expectantly for me to reply. Not only did she sound like a schoolmarm, but she looked the part, too. Her glasses were perched on the end of her nose and her Dutch-boy haircut framed her round face.

I told her I understood, and she began to ask me a series of questions: Please describe the alleged harassment. Did anyone else see it? Have you noticed your supervisor treating you differently than the other members of the department? How is your working relationship with the other men in your department? When she finished the questions, she asked me if there was anything else I would like to add.

The questions were not what I expected. I asked her what she planned on doing next. Pearce said she would be "interviewing" Cochran and other members of the department including Dino and Conshafter. She said she would be getting back to me.

When I returned to my department, I noticed that no one was speaking to me. Everyone who passed me, turned the other way. I felt as if I were the invisible woman. I was pretty sure I couldn't expect much—if any—support from my coworkers. Even if they felt like being supportive, I doubted that they would be allowed to express their feelings to me. Cochran, Conshafter and Dino were their bosses, too. They weren't about to jeopardize their own positions for a problem they knew nothing about. The tension within our department had definitely reached an all-time high.

I wondered at this point whether anyone in the station's other departments even knew this drama was transpiring. I suspected they didn't, because everyone in the newsroom and the other areas of the station seemed to be behaving normally toward me. I suspected that only my department had been told about the investigation.

When I returned to my desk after meeting with Sue Pearce, I had more interoffice mail. At the rate they are going, I thought, they had better reorder their corporate stationery:

October 26, 1981

Dear Kathy:

You're invited to participate in our continuing investigation concerning the charges of sexual harassment against Tom Cochran.

We are concerned about the allegations and at this stage no lawyers are to be involved from either side during the investigation.

Whether or not you participate, the investigation will continue.

Should you choose not to participate, you must understand that a decision could be made based upon all other interviews.

Sincerely.

Paul "Dino" Dinovitz
Vice President and
General Manager

On Wednesday morning, I asked Sue Pearce if I could talk to her again. I was uncomfortable with her questions. They were very targeted, and I felt as though they really didn't give her enough information to do a thorough investigation regarding my experience with sexual harassment. Something wasn't right. Most of her questions seemed to be about my behavior and not Cochran's.

I had just finished writing an order for a client when Jim Conshafter came over to my desk and asked that I come into his office. Already seated in Jim's office was the director of community relations, Joe Lentini.

Jim went behind his desk, but remained standing. "We are asking you to leave the building. You are going on a leave of absence for a week," said Jim. Lentini said nothing. Apparently he was there either as a witness or to serve as moral support for Jim. I guessed the real reason for his presence was probably the latter.

I hadn't expected this. Although I thought I was prepared for everything, it had never occured to me that they would temporarily throw me out of the station.

"I don't want to go on a leave of absence," I told him. "I have work to do—there are orders on my desk that need to be placed. What about my clients?" I asked. "May I call them and tell them I'm going to be out?"

Jim was like a robot, his face was like stone. "You have no choice in this matter. We will handle your clients. We will take care of the orders that need to be placed. You are to leave the building and not have any contact with your clients while you are on your leave of absence. You are also not to take anything with you that belongs to Channel 2. We are in the process of conducting business here, and you are not to interfere." I noticed, as Sue Pearce had done, he also was reading from a piece of paper.

I asked him if he was making Cochran take a leave of absence as well.

"No," came his firm and quick reply. "As far as we are concerned, there is no reason to make Tom take a leave of absence." He saw me to the front lobby of the building. He was walking so fast behind me, I was half-expecting him to give me a push right out the door.

Before going out, I stopped and turned to him. I wanted to reason with him. "Jim, please. Is this necessary? I have orders on my desk that need to be placed." I was almost pleading.

He was impatient and had no intention of having any sort of conversation with me. "I said we would deal with that," he told me, finally. "It is not your problem."

I stood outside for a minute trying to think of a way to somehow restore my dignity. I must look so foolish right now, standing outside of my office and not being allowed to go back in. I took a deep breath, trying to think of where I should go. While I was pondering my next step, to make a bad moment worse, I noticed out of the corner of my eye that two figures were standing in Cochran's office looking out the window at me. Conshafter and Cochran were both watching me leave. I quickly walked to my car.

My leave of absence gave me a week to devote all my energy to worrying myself sick about what was going to happen when I went back to work. I did nothing except go over again and again the events that had taken place during the preceding weeks.

I could only imagine what was going on at the station while I was doing my "sentence." I could just picture them going through my desk, fingering my files, reading my notes—invading what had been my own corner of the world.

But as much as I worried about what was happening at Channel 2, I was equally concerned about what my clients were thinking. My unscheduled absence had to be puzzling and perhaps even annoying to them.

Because of this nagging concern, one of my close friends volunteered to place a call to the station while I listened in. She asked for me by name, and the secretary said I wasn't in—at the moment. My friend said it was urgent and could she leave a message? The secretary said she could, and that I would get right back to her.

Now I was really worried. What Jim Conshafter had told me was not true. They weren't taking care of my work. My clients would think I was being delinquent by not responding to or returning their calls. I had some fast explaining to do when I went back.

On November 4th, I returned to work.

Right at 9 a.m. Cochran called me into his office and said he was pulling me off two of my accounts. During the past week, both clients had expressed their dissatisfaction with my work to him. He said that I had not returned their phone calls. It appeared that both of those clients had placed orders with me the week before, and that the schedules had not run. I wasn't surprised. He didn't need to tell me who the unhappy clients were—their orders were the ones I had left on my desk the day I was sent out the door on my leave of absence.

When I got back to my desk, I just sat there. I was waiting for the next reprimand, the next shot, the next person to tell me what I had done. I found it impossible to do any work. It seemed too difficult to concentrate on a job that was in the process of being destroyed.

I didn't have to wait long for the next play. Sue Pearce called me into her office and told me she had just about completed her "impartial" investigation and that she would be notifying me of the outcome shortly. She seemed self-satisfied. I didn't like the look on her face; she reminded me of the Cheshire cat.

At 4 p.m, Jim Conshafter called me in to his office and handed me a letter.

November 4, 1981

Dear Kathleen,

This will serve as a notice of your termination by WGR-TV, effective immediately. You are separated for poor work performance, a matter which has been brought to your attention repeatedly by members of the WGR Management.

With regard to your claims concerning Tom Cochran, we have carefully investigated those claims and all relevant evidence presented by you and others relating to those claims. We find your claims to be without merit.

Yours truly,

James Conshafter
General Sales Manager
WGR-TV, Channel 2

After reading the letter, I looked up at Jim. His eyes looked very small behind his glasses. His jaw was locked tight. "May I collect my personal things?" I asked. I felt empty and ashamed. I had never been fired before. I had not only lost a job I loved, but I had been denied something that meant even more: the right to say no to something I found offensive.

I was shaken. What was I going to do for work? What would I tell people? I tried to fight the instant desperation that was taking over. I had to be strong—I had to handle this. It wasn't the end of the world—it just felt like it. It was just a job, I told myself. There are worse tragedies. But it wasn't just a job—it was my job. And I had lost it.

I left Jim Conshafter's office for the last time.

As I mechanically gathered my personal items from my desk, I overheard Jim Conshafter call the other members of the team together for a quick meeting in "Tommy's" office.

With my philodendron plant carelessly tucked sideways under my arm and trying to balance the remainder of my things under my other arm, I walked by the open door of Cochran's office. By this time, the entire department was sitting there, including Tom and Jim. No one was making a sound. Although all of them saw me leave, no one dared acknowledge me.

I got into my car and the thought immediately hit me that I had no business having a new car because, now that I was out of work, I didn't know how I was going to be able to pay for it. It slowly dawned on me that my life was going to be very different from now on—or at least until I could find another job.

Despite my overwhelming feelings of shame and anger, I felt a certain relief that the past four months were finally over. Although I had always thought of myself as a strong person, I knew that I couldn't have withstood much more adversity. The sexual harassment, the hostility from my boss, Jim Conshafter letting me down, the sham of an investigation, the cold appearance of my coworkers, and then the firing—it had been a lot to handle.

Maybe now that the harassment was over I could start to accept what had happened to me. While I was working, I was consumed by my need to stay alert—always needing to be ready to duck and dodge—I hadn't been able to let down my guard for a minute. Now I could stop looking over my shoulder. No one was after me anymore.

It was really hard to believe that just a few months ago everything had been great: I had received a good job offer from another station, I had received some community and professional recognition, I had had a good life.

Now it was only the fourth of November, and I was cast in an entirely new role. I was an outcast—a loser—shamefully fired from my job for alleged poor performance. My claims against my supervisor had been found to be without merit, so I guess that made me a liar as well. The "Blue Angels" flying team couldn't have made that spectacular of a nosedive.

What a difference a few months of sexual harassment can make in your life, I thought woefully, as I drove to my lawyer's office to ask him what I was supposed to do next.

Chapter 5

Fighting Back

Alice had never been in a court of justice before, but she had read about them in books; and she was quite pleased to find that she knew the name of nearly everything there.

Alice's Adventures in Wonderland
Lewis Carroll

I didn't want to fight back. God knew, the last thing I wanted to be involved in was a legal battle. But I was sure I couldn't live with myself if I did nothing. While I was employed at Channel 2, even after months of being sexually harassed, I never had any intention of going to court. I wanted to continue working for Channel 2—I wanted to keep my career—I did not want to sue my employer. But after being fired, I had nowhere else to go but to court. Something very wrong had happened to me. I needed someone else to help make it right.

I didn't have any idea what the legal process would require of me emotionally, physically, and certainly not financially. I found the mere thought of going to federal court unimaginable. And, yet, without really ever having any tangible clues as to what the outcome would be, I made an unbreakable promise to myself, that no matter what lay ahead of me, no matter how long it took, I would keep going—I would see it through.

It was like a startling revelation—a deeply personal awakening to a more profound side of our modern reality. Overnight, I went from having a rather rosy view of life as that which is seen only by those who have miraculously been spared from strife, to a sudden and jolting exposure to the panorama of sights that can only be seen from life's sometimes cruel and heartless frontline.

Nothing would ever be the same.

I suddenly understood the passion of men and women who cry out about the injustices that plague our society and the motivations of those who respond freely to the need for human rights and who struggle unfalteringly toward the triumph of good over evil. I abruptly realized what made ordinary people—those living with the absence of power, position, or money—find the courage to say no to things they don't believe in. I discovered where those other "little" people found the unflinching faith and endless conviction required to stand up—and stand alone—for the sake of what they *did* believe in, even at the terrible and likely risk of everything else in their lives falling apart. There became no question in my mind that those who chose to speak up found their strength in simply doing what they believed was right. I was sure of it, because that is where I had found mine.

All of this was new to me, for controversy had previously been a stranger. Up until this tumultuous time in my life, I had only talked about what I believed in—I never expected that I would have to fight for it, too. For me, it no longer became just an employee/employer dispute under the court file label of *Neville* v. *Taft Broadcasting*. It wasn't just my own fate I had become concerned with—something much bigger seemed at stake. It had clearly become a head-to-head confrontation about something more important; a much larger drama was about to be played out, one that had far more implications and truly greater significance than my own singular and personal pain. And my direction on the course I had chosen seemed to have come from within. The powerful little voice that exists in each of us, no matter how much we try to ignore or silence it, always gets heard. And mine refused to be silent; it pressed and taunted me to fight back.

Finally, it all just simply came down to the fact that I had no choice. So I made my decision to fight and I did it wholeheartedly and without regret. From that point on, I couldn't—and I wouldn't—look back.

February 1982

My lawyer was talking, and I was trying to take careful notes in the notebook I had labeled "lawsuit." I was forcing myself to concentrate on each and every word Joe said, but I was dead tired, and my thoughts kept going to the hospital where my father lay critically ill. Two weeks earlier, he had suffered a severe stroke. Having been the first of my family to arrive at the emergency room, I stood in quiet shock by my father's bed while the soft-spoken priest quietly murmured the last rights. While the priest prayed for mercy, I asked God to forget the mercy—for now—and let him live a little longer. Thankfully, it was my prayer that was answered that night.

The doctors were surprised that he managed to survive, but even though he was holding on, his overall prognosis was not good. He was partially paralyzed and now needed his family to help him recover enough to be able to lead some sort of life. If he recovered, it wouldn't be easy for him and it would certainly be hard on my mother.

I couldn't help but think of my four brothers and how my father's illness would change all of our lives. We had always been such a close family. It seemed as though no one in our family could make a move without the others knowing exactly what was going on. And my father was not the head of the family, he was the center. While growing up, all of us, including my mother, had adapted to and even flourished within his rather easy and unconventional ways of raising a family. Like his own father, who was an Irish immigrant, my dad believed that our home must be open—at all times—to anyone and anything that was standing (or sitting) outside the door. Although we had pedigreed dogs, my father seemed to prefer the sorry-looking strays that wandered into our lives missing pieces of their wagging tails. My mother finally had to tell my dad that his "good heart" was getting out of control when one of his moody adoptees, Spooky, would not allow any human beings, including those of us who lived there, to enter the house.

My father delighted in the fact that all during their high school and college years, my four brothers brought home the tennis, basketball, football, baseball, wrestling, and track teams, various chapters of fraternities, and portions of dormitories for the weekend or however long they wished to say. If I wasn't home by a reasonable hour, my bedroom would often already be taken up by a tight end or linebacker. A packed house paid off for me when I was little, I sold 54 boxes of Girl Scout cookies—in a matter of days—and never once had to leave the house.

Because there were always "guests" around our house, my father was known for moving through the bedrooms between 5:30 and 6 a.m. on Saturday mornings shaking shoulders to ask someone what his name was, what sport he played, whether he liked Notre Dame, and whether he wanted to have breakfast with him. Plain and simple—my father loved having kids around. Now, the last of his sons was a junior at Cornell University and his sudden illness would probably mean that he wouldn't live to see Jim graduate.

Like most adult children, I had accepted the reality that someday I had to face the inevitable pain of losing my parents. But I didn't want that time to be now, while I was involved in such an awful and seemingly stupid thing. Even though he had often confided to my mother that he was pretty sure he was attending the exact same show over and over again, my father had cheerfully suffered through all of my dance recitals and concerts and pageants throughout the years and had tried hard not to miss my more "significant" appearances on television. He had been a good father to me and now I had nothing to show him. If this was the end of his life, I felt as though I had let him down.

With my father ill, all I really wanted to do was spend a good deal of time with my family, but, unfortunately, I was committed to finishing a lawsuit that I had started. And I couldn't forget that I also needed to keep looking for a job. I was beginning to wonder if the cynics were on to something when they quickly quipped that life isn't always fair. If that statement had any truth to it, I was pretty certain it would also ring true when a person got entangled in a sexual harassment lawsuit.

Every day the suit against Channel 2 brought new complications into my life. I had been out of work for four months now, and still hadn't found another job. I was already well into my savings and was becoming worried about my financial situation.

Although the story about my being fired from my job had been in the *Buffalo News*, I tried to remain optimistic about its impact on my future employment in the area. I felt certain I could explain the circumstances under which I was fired adequately to a prospective employer. I found out soon enough that my situation was *not* such an easy thing to explain. And, to my surprise, many people knew all about it and had already drawn their own conclusions.

When someone I had known professionally treated me differently and perhaps seemed a little withdrawn, I kept telling myself that I was just being overly sensitive. He wasn't really looking at me oddly, I supposed, I only *thought* he was behaving strangely. At first, I acted on the assumption that my brush with controversy was only a temporary outburst, and soon my real and normal life would spring back from its hiding place. Somehow, I had counted on people being more accepting about what had happened to me. I was also relying on the passage of time to diminish the attention my adversity had acquired. I was hoping that people would simply forget it had happened. I was confident that very soon my tangle with harassment would be yesterday's news. But, as it turned out, I was wrong.

Evidently, any rumble of a story that has the words "television" and "sex" connected to it makes great gossip. Suddenly and from seemingly everyone, I heard bits and pieces of all kinds of sketchy rumors about myself that easily could have made my hair stand on end if I had heard them myself. It staggered me that people were discussing me on buses, at bars, in their offices, and even at their dinner tables. When I had tried to report for unemployment insurance, I found that even there, I was forced to face up to my new notoriety. I cringed when the young clerk at the window exclaimed, "Hey, I recognize you. Aren't you the one who. . ."

Yes, I was the one.

Although Buffalo was the 32nd largest market in the country, it seemed to be an exceedingly small town when it came to rumor circulation in the working community. I went on countless interviews over the months I was unemployed and continued to find that news of my involvement in a "sexual harassment scandal" had already preceded me. After the interviewer spent several minutes curiously prying details out of me as to what exactly happened at Channel 2, I would try to spend the rest of the time steering the interview back to my consideration for the job for which I was applying. But no jobs were ever offered. The controversy and publicity surrounding my discharge from Channel 2 had made me too hot to hire.

I realized, however, that it wasn't just my departure from Channel 2 that made prospective employers reluctant to hire me; the fact that I was suing my former employer didn't exactly add exciting new skills to my resume. Suing a company you worked for isn't something you would want to list as one of your hobbies on your curriculum vitae. Hobbies and Outside Interests: tennis, horseback riding, flower arranging and—oh, yes—litigating. I was an untouchable who was doing the unthinkable. Some Career Woman of the Year, I thought bleakly.

Once, again, irony had struck. So much for my being able to help young women find promising careers through my "able" leadership of the Women in Touch program, I thought miserably. I was the woman no company would touch. But lawsuit or no lawsuit, I needed a job—and I needed it quickly.

Joe's voice brought me back to the present. He was walking around his office as though he was in front of a jury, trying to convince its members of his client's innocence. "We have a lot of work ahead of us and some things, unless we address them now, could be problematical. Although I have never actually tried a case like this before, as a criminal attorney I can tell you we'll have our hands full," he stretched his open palms to make his point, "when it comes to taking this one to court."

He straightened his suspenders. As always, he was impeccably dressed. Joe was a well-known face in the legal community and had a solid reputation in the field of criminal law. I hoped he would do equally well in the area of law that concerned my case. I certainly knew nothing about employment or discrimination law. I was counting on him.

He went on. "This is an overwhelming effort—your action against Channel 2. As the plaintiff, you have the burden of proof and you have a couple of important things that need to be proven. And, if I understand the process correctly," he was emphasizing each word artfully, "it is a long one."

"Our filing of your complaint with the Equal Employment Opportunity Commission a few weeks ago is just the beginning. After we receive our right-to-sue letter from the EEOC, then we can proceed with the next step: filing our claim in federal court." He was almost thinking out loud at this point. "I've become convinced that the best thing to do is to go straight to federal court; we'll have a judge hear this case. In fact, I've discussed this case with some colleagues of mine, and they think a non-jury trial is the best way to go." He explained his logic further. "Just a judge will hear it. It'll be faster in the long run and judges are keenly attuned to the law, whereas jurors are sometimes not. Anyway, that's the direction I think we should take. That is, if it gets to trial, and, hopefully, it won't get that far."

He continued, "As I mentioned to you when we filed your EEOC complaint, I thought it best that we not bother suing Cochran personally, athough we could have, I suppose. He assaulted you, for sure, but if we go after him, we'd have to go through the state courts. This way, by just filing through Title VII, we will be taking civil action but not criminal action and we will only need to deal with federal court. It's cleaner this way. It would be more troublesome suing both Cochran and Channel 2. And as far as I'm concerned, our real complaint is with Channel 2 management, anyway. They are the ones who ultimately did you the most harm.

"Now, as far as the problems we need to address in this case," said Joe, "we have to prove a couple of important things. A, we have to prove that they had no real reason to fire you, and B," he raised his index finger and pointed it into the air, "we have to show that, in fact, Cochran did it: that he harassed you." He seemed satisfied with his perspective on things. "And that, my dear, is our basic case."

I kept listening.

"As we get into the guts of the litigation, the first part of our burden could, and probably will, resemble the piles of paper that accompany an antitrust suit into court. The research will be long and tedious. Prior to even drawing the necessary conclusions, the documentation and paperwork alone is going to be overwhelming. Now, that's where *you* come in." He directed his wide gestures to me.

"Because you can't possibly come up with the money to support the hourly rates this effort would demand to engage me—or any of my associates, for that matter—to perform the kind of thorough research this litigation will require, I will be looking to *you* to pull together the basic elements that will support our trial strategy." He gave me a challenging look. "You are going to play an important role in your own case. Now, normally I don't ask clients to become so involved in their own litigation but we have special circumstances here. With our limitations on resources and because you are obviously so bright, I know I can count on you to assist me greatly in preparing this case for trial—in the event that it makes it that far. You can be a great help. And no one knows the business you were in like *you* do."

At this point, I knew what Joe was attempting to do. He wanted me to feel important so that I would do the things he didn't have time—or didn't want—to do.

But, Joe didn't need to make me feel intrinsically significant, nor did he need to motivate me to perform the tedious tasks that would obviously be required of me. I had correctly assumed I would be a working and productive plaintiff. I was certainly willing to do anything to help win the case. And, most important, because I wanted everything done right, it was to my ultimate advantage that I stay closely involved in all the details of the suit. I didn't care how much time it would take me or how much overwhelming drudgery there would be; I would see to it that we had all the essential and accurate documentation and facts needed to prove my position.

And Joe had made a valid point. I was familar with all the records at Channel 2. On the bright side, I would get a pretty good education about law while I was involved in this litigation business.

Something about my case was already gnawing at me. A brand-new young lawyer, who had just passed the bar a few weeks before, had prepared my EEOC complaint. When he had asked me to sign it I had mentioned to him that it wasn't exactly the whole story on paper. He was untroubled by my concern and was quick to tell me that I would have a chance to tell all the details at trial. I hadn't liked the fact that he really hadn't addressed my question. Perhaps it would be better if I stayed completely involved in everything that went on at the law office. Then someone would have to answer my questions. And I was sure I would have plenty of questions.

Joe was enthusiastically listing my first assignments, "Put together a complete list of station records we need to subpoena that will give you the exact figures and information you need to prove later, in court, that you were as good as the next guy at the station. During discovery we will subpoena everything we need from them—and we also will have to develop a set of interrogatories and," he took a breath, "we need to start doing depositions—starting with Cochran. I will also need you to prepare a list of everyone else we should examine before trial, including background information on those people. And, those asinine complaints Cochran had about you attending that Wilson deal and those two client complaints that supposedly took place while you were on the forced leave of absence—you will have to think about how you want to respond to those. And, we have to find out who fired you—was it Cochran or was it Conshafter—or did both of them do it—together? I, personally, find that an interesting question."

He made it sound like a game of "Clue," and I was the victim who got nailed with the lead pipe in the conservatory. He was standing up again, with all the stance and moves of a true defender of the law.

"Like I said," he finally noted, as he half-spun away from his window to face me, his hands clasped together in front of him "this is unquestionably an arduous task. There is substantial work to be done, and I am going to be counting on you to do a great deal of it. By the way, how is your father doing, and how is the job search coming along?"

"Okay," I answered thoughtfully, "I'll begin immediately to make a list of all the documents that need to be ordered and I'll also begin compiling information that can be used in our first set of interrogatories." I wouldn't let him down.

The lawsuit had really begun.

May 1982

The telephone calls in the middle of the night had started even before the EEOC complaint had been filed. Because I lived alone, and because they were death threats, just hearing them whispered over the phone more than succeeded in scaring me half to death. Although I thought they were a ridulous tactic for someone to use, I still couldn't shake off the eerie feeling they gave me.

Now that my father was in poor health and had been moved from the hospital to a nursing/rehabilitation center in Clarence, New York, I jumped to answer the phone when it rang in the middle of the night. I was always afraid the call might be about him. Although I was relieved when it wasn't, I would immediately become wide awake and terrified when I recognized the raspy voice. I didn't know who the caller was, but I surely knew what he wanted. His annoying and unsettling calls never brought him his desired result, however. Instead, he made me more determined to proceed with the lawsuit. No one was ever going to threaten me again.

Unfortunately, I could never get back to sleep after the calls, and they happened frequently enough to make me lose a great deal of sleep. I knew the calls would stop once the trial was over. But until then, I would just lie there many nights waiting for morning to come. During those times, I would comfort myself by telling myself how everything would get back to normal—once the trial was over. *Then* things would be better.

Not all the calls I got during the days after I was fired were death threats.

One morning, I got a call that not only took me completely by surprise but also offered a much-needed bit of hope. The call came from Molly McCoy, the nightly news anchor for Channel 2. I sat in stunned silence as Molly proceeded to tell me why she was calling. "I've been so worried about you. When I didn't see you around the station, I finally started asking people questions. No one in your department would tell me what had happened to you. Everyone was acting strangely. Something seemed so wrong. When I heard why you were really gone, I knew I had to get in touch with you. I had to tell you that it happened to me, too."

At first, I wasn't sure what she was saying. What could have happened to her?

Molly McCoy was a wide-eyed and beautiful "Texan girl" who had become a favorite face on TV for many Buffalo viewers. She and I had met five years earlier when I was a regular guest on her "2 at Noon" magazine show. As fashion director for L.L. Berger's, I used to bring along models, and Molly and I would discuss on-air the new trends in fashion and home furnishings. We found that we worked easily together and quickly developed a mutual respect for each other. But other than once attending the ballet with Molly, I really didn't know her on a personal level, so I was puzzled as to what she was referring to—now.

"Cochran," she said firmly and without hesitation. " He did the same thing to me." She went on hurriedly. "The only thing different about my situation is that I don't work for him—thank goodness. I can't even stand to see him at the station. I've avoided him ever since it happened. Now I won't let him get within three feet of me." She rushed on, "I'm so sorry I didn't know about your problem while you still worked here. But hopefully I can be some help to you now. What I want from you," she said deliberately, "is your lawyer's name and telephone number. I'm going to call your attorney, right now, and tell him I'd like to make a statement. You weren't alone in this. You had company. I'm sure if it happened to us, it happened to others. In fact, I'm sure if we checked around, I'd say there were definitely other women he bothered."

For the first time since everything had started, I no longer felt so completely alone. Although I had an interested lawyer and wonderfully supportive friends, I often felt as if no one else understood what I was feeling. Now, there was someone else who I knew understood. And, I agreed with Molly. I had more than suspected that Cochran's pattern with women had been repeated with others besides Molly and me.

Seven months after I left Channel 2, I got a job. The offer came from my old boss. My previous employer, L.L. Berger's asked me to help them execute a major sales promotion effort that would include opening a new store, writing and producing a television and radio campaign, and producing a number of special events and live shows. My old boss Louis Berger, president of the store chain needed some help and, certainly, so did I. The project kept me employed for six months.

While I was working for Berger's, my lawsuit was filed with federal court in Buffalo, and, once again, I made the news. Unfortunately, Joe did not have the opportunity to tell me it was going to hit, so when a local televison anchorman called me one afternoon, I didn't realize what he meant when he said he wanted me to comment further on the filing.

"Boy, when you do things, you do them right," he remarked lightly.

"What do you mean?" I asked. These days I wasn't so sure whether I was doing anything right.

"You mean you haven't seen tonight's paper? It's a good-sized article. In fact, right now, we're considering opening with the story on the 6 p.m. news."

Finally, he realized that I didn't know anything about the article so he detailed it for me quickly. "Well, let me read some of it to you," he offered. "According to this article, you are suing for $800,000." He continued to read, but I gently cut him off and thanked him for calling me.

I ran out of my office. I had to get an evening paper and find out what I was doing these days.

I stumbled upon some more "news" about myself during the six months I worked at Berger's.

One day, the vice president of personnel for the store chain asked me to stop by her office when I had a minute. I wasn't concerned that she wanted to meet with me. I often met with the head of personnel regarding additional staffing needs that I required to implement various programs I was currently managing. She was extremely accommodating and also liked to stay well informed of any of the marketing efforts coming out of my department.

During the first time I had worked for L.L. Berger's, prior to leaving the company for the position at Channel 2, the director of personnel and I had enjoyed an excellent working relationship. Together, we had both been responsible for training all employees in all sales promotion efforts for the ten-store specialty goods retail chain. Sandy was extremely verbal and always blunt when it came to making a point.

"Hi, Neville, how are you and sit down. I got a really strange call a little while ago that I thought I'd better tell you about," she said all in one breath. "At first, I wasn't going to tell you because I know you are going crazy with all the stuff you're working on now, and I know you're worried about your dad and, well, I also know the lawsuit is really bogging you down. I hated to add one more thing to the pile, but the more I thought about it, the more I thought I'd better tell you. If I were you, I'd want to know something like this."

She was preparing me for something. It wasn't like Sandy to beat around the bush like this.

She paused, "Okay, let me just put it this way—if I *didn't* know you like I *do* know you—you wouldn't be working here, right now."

"Sandy, what are you talking about?" I asked impatiently. "Is someone here at the store upset about the litigation with Channel 2?"

Even though I was only back at Berger's to manage the marketing effort until the new store was opened, I continually worried about my lawsuit making waves. I felt there was a stigma attached to me, and I always had my ear out for any rumbling of discomfort felt by other members of the management team. Because I was currently heading up all of the store's marketing efforts, I served on the ten-member management team that ran the company. Being so close to things, I thought I would have picked up on any internal problems my lawsuit might have created. I had been grateful to the president of the company for being so understanding of my situation. But I had other reasons to be grateful to Louis Berger. He had been the only person in the community to call and offer me a job after I had been fired from Channel 2. Because he was comfortable with my decision, I felt that he had made it easier for the other members of the management team to accept—and then forget—that I was involved in litigation. I hoped Sandy wasn't telling me that my presumption was wrong. I didn't think I could handle it.

"Well, I got a call—right out of the blue—from the community relations director at Channel 2. The call was about you," her voice dropped. "I could tell he didn't know you were back here working with us, so I didn't let on at first. He told me he knew you used to work here before you went to Channel 2, and he asked me what kind of work you did while you were here. I told him Mr. Berger thought the world of you and that you were a good employee—you know, I told him you were creative, hard-working—blah blah—you know—all of that. But after I went on about you, I asked him why he was inquiring. After all, I seriously doubted he was asking me to give you some sort of recommendation—which he got whether he wanted one or not."

"Anyway he had a lot to say about you. He told me you had made some very serious and false accusations about a manager there. That you had been nothing but trouble for this poor guy and that you had, in fact, created quite a stir within their organization." She stopped for a minute, seemingly becoming impatient with herself for being so diplomatic. She leaned forward and slapped her hand on the desk in front of her, "Look, let me just put it this way—the guy was not flattering when it came to discussing you. Had I gotten that call, and not already known what kind of person—and employee—you are, I certainly wouldn't hire you off the street. But, thank God, I do know you."

"Listen, Neville—the call really made me mad. I began

to wonder who else this guy was calling." She shook her head sympathically. "This is a pretty ugly thing for you, isn't it? Is there anything I can do?"

I told Sandy I wasn't surprised at what she had told me and that I guessed that kind of behavior could be expected when one is going up against a company in court. I thanked her for letting me know and left her office.

But I was surprised that Channel 2 had stooped so low, I thought as I stepped onto the elevator. And I was fully aware, now, that they weren't playing by the rules. I had been under the impression that we were going to meet in court and fight it out there. But, obviously, I was wrong. And I couldn't believe the man who called would do something like that. It had been less than a year earlier that the same man had nominated me for a community service award. I was the only person at Channel 2 he had recommended. In fact, I still had his note attached to his nomination and I remembered precisely what he had written across the top of the award form: *Tom C: Neville should be considered for this—she would be perfect.*

As I got off the elevator and headed back to my office, I realized I must accept the fact that my battle with Channel 2 was not going to begin and end in court. Whether I liked it or not, it had become a part of my life.

Chapter 6

Right Day-Wrong Tea Party

"Take some more tea," the March Hare said to Alice, earnestly.
"I've had nothing yet," Alice replied in an offended tone: "so I can't take more."
"You mean you can't take less," said the Hatter. "It's very easy to take more than nothing."

Alice's Adventure
in Wonderland
Lewis Carroll

April 1983

"I'm not going to do it. It's a ridiculous request, Joe," I shook my head angrily, "and I fail to see what it has to do with anything. Just tell them I won't do it."

It was the first day of my examination before trial, and Joe and I were in the conference room of Channel 2's local law firm. I had already testified for almost seven hours and I was getting tired. Now, Joe had just told me that the

Taft attorneys wanted to see all of the trophies and awards I had won from the time I was in college.

Already the Taft attorneys had managed to get Joe to agree to hand over my daily appointment/diary book that I had used during my last year at Channel 2. As my deposition continued, elsewhere in the law firm a young associate was busy having the hour-by-hour account of my personal and business appointments duplicated. The appointment book also contained a great many personal reminders which were kept for my eyes only. I had made a grave mistake when I had referred to it to verify a date earlier in the morning session of the deposition. Once the Taft attorneys spotted it in my hand, they immediately requested it from Joe.

And now they wanted to see my trophies.

"They actually want me to bring in my hardware—here, to this room?" I whispered incredulously to Joe. I couldn't imagine why Taft was interested in seeing my trophies and awards that were now stashed away somewhere at my parents' house. Aside from the fact that it was completely irrelevant, I resented the request. Behind each of those trophies were young and cherished memories complete with dance shoes and costumes and gowns and glitter. My years in stage competition, particularly in the Miss America program, had been both rigorous and rewarding. And the road I had taken had not been dull. I had had dance teachers and modeling coaches and speech teachers from one side of the state to the other. My training had been disciplined, my teachers had been carefully selected, my approach had always been determined. And after having won more than a dozen scholarships from the Miss New York and Miss Connecticut programs, I had happily hung up my own performance shoes and begun to train other young women with an even greater enthusiasm than I had put into my own effort. With all my heart I loved to dance and I was delighted to be around younger women who felt the same way. Of course, I fully realized now—and even back then—that those who criticize such competitions have a good argument. In fact I would never even attempt to debate someone on whether such programs are substantially relevant in the big scheme of life. I had always readily agreed that pageants are a bit on the corny side—but didn't that also hold true for so many other contests which serve to preserve the important quest of the American dream? I had always assumed that that was the whole point of striving to win SuperBowl rings and Olympic gold medals and the World Series and even Miss America. Those who attained the goal of being named champions—and even those who had only tried—kept the dream alive and going strong. They were important reminders. So, although I had accumulated a substantial collection of trophies, it was the memory that I had of "going for it" that mattered to me now—not the remaining pieces of metal still life that the Taft lawyers wanted to see.

But apparently it was more than the trophies the attorneys were requesting. They also wanted to see all of the newspaper clippings regarding any publicity I had received over the years and any scrapbooks that had been kept on the more notable moments of my life. And they specifically requested to see the display that had hung on the walls of my high school's library when I had been honored in 1981, the same year I was fired—the year that now seemed so long ago.

They also wanted any and all records regarding the formation of the group, "Women in Touch," which I had founded. They were particularly interested as to how I had handled the financial matters of the volunteer group.

They wondered if I had claimed any tax write-off on my own personal income taxes. Could I bring those documents in, too, they asked Joe.

Joe didn't want me to get upset and be unreasonable in front of the Taft attorneys. I had already demanded that only one of the defense attorneys be allowed to remain in the room while I answered questions about my health, including specific interrogation about my gynecological history. I had absolutely nothing to hide, as all of them already knew. Prior to my deposition, they had carefully studied my entire medical records going back to when I was only five years old. I had not budged an inch when it came to refusing to address a roomful of Taft attorneys while I was being questioned about my medical history. It was hard enough answering their questions considering the fact that the Taft attorneys had invited the new general manager of Channel 2 and Tom Cochran, himself, to sit in on my deposition.

Thank God, my medical records were very boring. I could only wonder what kind of questioning I would have had to endure had they not been. It was easy to see that they were searching for flaws in my character or background, and they seemed intent upon finding something.

But, in this instance, I was going to remain firm when it came to avoiding making a circus act out of the personal memorabilia of my life. "Joe, I'm not going to my parents' house and haul my trophies here. Forget it—no trophies." I folded my arms tightly in front of me to indicate that I was through talking about the matter.

Joe left me to confer with the Taft attorneys. I really had to suppress an uncontrollable urge to laugh. The situation was absurd; corporate attorneys conferring with a criminal lawyer regarding the transporting and displaying of a plaintiff's trophies had to be a new exercise for these lawyers. Or perhaps it wasn't, I reconsidered cynically.

"Okay, we're going to compromise," said Joe eagerly. "You don't have to bring your trophies in," he said triumphantly, "but you do have to bring in your scrapbooks and plaques—and they definitely want to see the stuff that was on the walls from 'Kathy Neville' day or whatever the heck it was."

Oh, great, I thought, sarcastically, what a deal.

After a full day of facing nonstop interrrogation by Taft's smooth lead counsel, I left the law firm and headed to the hospital. My father had been moved back into intensive care and he wasn't doing well. This time I was more than a little concerned. It had been over a year since I had made my bargain with God asking that we be allowed to keep him a little longer. I was afraid that time was running out.

That night, after leaving my family at the hospital, I went home to gather together the little mementos of my happier days, which the Taft attorneys had insisted on viewing the next day. The things I carefully placed in boxes were my own private treasures. I could hardly stand to touch the little bits and pieces of my past, knowing where I would be taking them in the morning. I resented what was happening—not only was my present life being ruined by the lawsuit, but now even my past was going to undergo the same shameful scrutiny.

The next day I waited outside the room while the attorneys circled the table where the items of my life were on display. I peeked in—it looked like a flea market—nothing more than a rummage table holding the pieces of my life, which they were now picking up and rolling over in their hands.

"Okay Miss Neville, you can take everything off the

table now," they called out to me. "And when you are through, we will resume the questioning." I didn't look at any of them while I put my things back in the box. I would never forget this moment, I thought bitterly. I could feel my lips begin to tighten as I continued to collect the items. Something very humiliating had just happened to me and I was the only one in the room who cared. Strangers were making a mockery out of life and doing it within the boundaries of legal practice, I thought, as I was sworn in by the court reporter.

The deposition resumed, and the questions didn't seem to stop. They asked me about my dancing lessons. "What *kind* of dancing did you do, Miss Neville? Exactly what *kind* of dancing was it?" asked the defense attorney expectantly. At times, I felt like giving him the ridiculous answers I thought he deserved, but, instead, I responded politely with the appropriate and accurate answers. "Ballet and jazz, Mr. Stewart. For 17 years I studied mostly ballet and jazz."

The questions were endless regarding my association with my old high school. The attorney wanted to know why there had been a "Kathy Neville Day." I wanted to tell him I wished to God there never had been one, but instead I told him I really didn't know.

The Taft attorneys came down hard on me when the deposition switched to questions about my performance. My head began to pound as I tried to recall exact details regarding specfic circumstances regarding a contract or a negotiation with a client. But if they thought I was going to break down during the depositions, they were wrong. One thing that I did pick up on very quickly was that breaking me was one of the purposes of such a thorough and grueling deposition. They were trying to find out what kind of witness I would be at trial. If I showed any signs of nervousness or became confused about the order of events, it would be a sign to them that I might fall apart at trial. I understood why they were applying all this pressure—and I wasn't about to show any strain.

Finally day two of my deposition, the questioning was over. The lawyers talked about needing at least one more day to question me, and they decided that it was convenient for them to do it the following week. I agreed reluctantly. It would mean I would have to take another day off from work, something I didn't really want to do.

I had finally gotten back into broadcasting, but it was a far cry from what I wanted to be doing. A local radio station had hired me the year before in a sales support position. Although my title was sales promotion director of the AM/FM station, the toughest part of my job frequently required me to swallow my pride. My main responsibility was to be available to serve miscellaneous needs of the account executives. I had taken a more than $28,000 yearly cut from what I would have earned during my last year at Channel 2. I was having a tough time living on my new earnings, and when account executives would impatiently ask me to order more balloons and helium for live remote promotions that they were doing for their clients, I had a very difficult time feeling good about my job.

In addition, my immediate boss was not very happy about my litigation with Channel 2. In fact, he made his feelings very clear. "If it had been only my decision, I never would have hired you," he announced to me one day. "I don't want someone who is involved in a court case working for me."

He certainly didn't need to tell me that, he had made those feelings evident in all his dealings with me. In fact, I was the only person on his staff who had to meet with him at the end of each day—and supply in written form a thorough accounting of every single second of my time. He required me to fill my daily plan out for him according to minutes of the day.

"If you are in the ladies room for three and a half minutes, I want to know about it," said my boss. "You must account for every single second and it must all add up." So each night I headed into his office with my daily summary sheets. I knew he was disappointed that I always had them ready for him. He was hoping that some night I wouldn't.

One of the men on the FM sales staff quietly watched as my boss continued to apply pressure to me. He finally told me he was upset about the way I was being treated. He confessed to me that he felt the treatment I was being subjected to was all because my boss didn't like the fact that I was involved in litigation with another broadcast station in town. He wondered if I agreed with his theory.

Without trying to sound like a martyr, I began to explain to Doug that I had learned to accept the fact that I was going to be treated differently by certain people because of my decision to go to court. I hated the way Michael, my boss, treated me, but I was going to endure it. I was not going to be out of a job.

"Doug, just for now, I *have* to take it," I explained, "I need this job and it will really be tough for me to go find another one, right now, particularly with all these pretrial things going on. I have no choice but to stick it out."

But what I didn't tell my coworker was that I hated my dead-end job. Just then, I was sick of everything. I was tired of the phone calls in the middle of the night, I hated not having any money, and I was weary of the lawsuit.

In May, my youngest brother graduated from Cornell University. I stayed behind at the hospital while my mother attended the graduation ceremonies in Ithaca. The fact that my youngest brother had finished his years of undergraduate schooling made me keenly aware that time was marching on. My frustration was mounting. I needed the lawsuit to be over. If I was ever going to have a career, again, I needed to get it behind me.

I started to push Joe for a trial date.

Pretrial discovery had gone on long enough, I told him. More than twenty depositions had been taken, hundreds of pages of documents had been filed with the courts, including extensive sets of interrogatories. I personally had put years into preparing documents. Things had to move faster, I stressed to Joe. I needed to get on with my life.

My father died a few days before Father's Day.

After his death, I became even more determined to get the litigation over and done with—I knew that life was too valuable to spend it fighting with a corporation. For some reason, the death threats stopped bothering me. Unemotionally, I got police protection and accepted them as a part of my daily life. I also began to accept the fact that, financially, things were going to be very tight for a long while. After having been out of work for such a long time and then finding a job that didn't even meet my expenses, not to mention the pressure of the financial commitment to the lawsuit — it was beginning to seem that there would never be a way out of the hole that had been dug for me after I had been fired from Channel 2. But like it or not, it was my new life and I slowly began to accept it.

But every day of my life seemed to be another test of patience and endurance. My social and professional life had become memories. There didn't seem to be any time or energy left in my daily life for pleasure. My friends had been very understanding when I just didn't have the strength to see them. One of the few things I managed to keep as a small part of my former life was my work in the community. I sensed it was more important than ever for me to stay involved in bigger things than my disagreement with Channel 2. I gladly directed the American Cancer Society show, taught the liturgical dance group at my church at Easter and Christmas and continued working with America's Junior Miss program. Although I no longer approached it with the same level of energy, the volunteer work gave my life some balance and offered a better perspective on my own problems. When I became preoccupied in projects that helped others, thankfully, things like court and sexual harassment seemed very far away. And the farther away those things were, the happier I was. I felt that being involved in a lawsuit could easily become an obsession. And there was no way *any* lawsuit was going to take over my life any more than it already had.

Six postponements later
July 1984

A year after my father died, the trial date had been postponed by Taft for the fourth time. This time, when I called Joe I was angry. Instead of getting him, I got his new associate, Louis.

"Louis I can't take any more. We cannot allow Taft to keep postponing the trial. It isn't right. Why are we letting them continue to do this?"

I knew I probably sounded like I was whining, but I didn't care. I was more upset than I had ever been, although I really wasn't being fair to this new attorney. He had been more than helpful during the six months he had been involved in the case. And I believed he understood what I was going through—he seemed to share my frustration. He had also become involved in the lawsuit at a time when it was clear that Joe was not as excited about the case as he once had been. I had noticed Joe's enthusiasm diminishing shortly before the end of the first year of the pretrial efforts. This being the third year, I knew Joe felt as though the case had become a huge albatross around his neck. It was no longer a fast-moving piece of litigation, it was a legal moose.

It was when I sensed that Joe had lost interest that I became even more determined to move things along. I told Joe I would do anything that needed to be done. Nothing was too trivial. I went to the law library and researched the latest decisions in Title VII. I completed hundreds of pages of research that could later be used in the trial. I wanted no stone unturned. I had to win the case—my whole professional future was riding on it.

"Louis, it has been almost four years! Yet, every time Taft asks for a postponement, we tell them no problem. You tell Joe—no more delays."

I hung up the phone and sighed. In a minute I would call Louis back and apologize. It wasn't his fault that the last postponement had been granted because Cochran's wife was pregnant, and that a sexual harassment trial would have been inconvenient for him at that time.

Missing: One Jim Conshafter

Jim Conshafter was a key person in my case. Even before I fully understood how a case like mine should be tried in court, I had known he was the one individual who would provide important testimony.

Jim Conshafter had hired me at Channel 2 and had always given me superior reviews. He was the person I had reported the harassment to in 1981. He was also the person who had fired me that same year.

After Jim Conshafter had testified in a pretrial deposition, I was anxious to read through all his testimony and find, in his own words, the reason he had given the record for firing me.

On a separate sheet of paper, I put all his testimony together regarding his decision to fire me, which seemed to point obviously to the fact that I had attended a luncheon at my former high school. And, just to get a clearer look at his testimony, I included any mention of managerial policy regarding the involvement of Channel 2 employees in community activities:

> **Conshafter:** Well, yes, attending outside events is encouraged. Salespeople get involved in community projects; they get involved in all types of things that bring them in contact with people in the business community.
>
> **Conshafter:** Cochran told me she [Neville] hadn't reported going [to the anti-drug luncheon] to anyone.
>
> **Conshafter:** I believe Cochran told me how long she [Neville] was gone [to the anti-drug luncheon] but I don't recall at this time.
>
> **Conshafter:** No, I never asked her [Neville] about it [the luncheon]. I was out of town.
>
> **Conshafter:** Cochran told me that she was at a function at her former high school with some other Channel 2 employees.
>
> **Conshafter:** In any event I learned of it [the luncheon], I believe, from our news director, he told our General Manager [Dino] at the time and he in fact talked to Cochran and we learned it through our news director.
>
> **Conshafter:** I did not speak to our news director [about the luncheon]. I think it was Cochran that got the information from the news director.

Conshafter: It was my impresson that she was gone for several hours. That's what Cochran said. I was out of town on that particular day.

Conshafter: I don't know if Kathy went out there on her lunch break or not, I don't know.

Conshafter: I'm not sure if she told the sales secretary, or not. I believe Cochran told me that she didn't.

Conshafter: No, there is no written policy or anything about [salespeople] letting them [management] know their whereabouts.

Conshafter: I had no reason to believe that Tom Cochran was telling me nothing but truthful information in this [luncheon] matter.

Conshafter: They [Cochran and the guys] could have been at the Quarterback Club. I was out of town that day [October 21].

Conshafter: I learned of Kathy's participation in the affair at her high school by a phone call I received on the 21st from Cochran. I was at my office in Chicago. He told me Kathy had an unexcused absence from the office. Cochran said she would not discuss it with him. I decided to terminate Kathy then, on the 21st, as a result of not being able to discuss her business with Tom and also because of an unexcused absence away from the station.

Conshafter: On [October 21] after hearing about the fact that she had attended [the luncheon]. That is when I made the decision to fire her. I told Cochran. . .I think we should terminate her.

To complete the picture I was seeing, I added one more bit of testimony to my collection of transcripts. After Joe had finished asking Conshafter about his reasons for firing me, allegedly due to my attending the Wilson Central School event, he asked Conshafter if he considered the possibility that Cochran might have been telling tales at this point in time, especially after I had reported Cochran's sexual advances to Conshafter. Conshafter simply replied that he had no opinion on that.

When it came to testifying in court, I thought Jim Conshafter's testimony would actually help me win my case. Knowing this, I was shocked when I found out that Jim Conshafter would not be a witness at the trial.

"How can he not be there?" I asked Louis, "Conshafter is supposedly the person who fired me! That's one of the two things this case is all about—whether I was harassed and why I got fired. Conshafter is critical to all of this."

I wanted Jim Conshafter at the trial. I knew he would have trouble seeing me in the courtroom while he was testifying. Evidently, Taft didn't want him there for the very reason that I did.

"But he's out of our reach, now," emphazied Louis.

Conshafter had since left Channel 2 and moved on to a station in Kansas City. And Dino had left Channel 2 when Taft had sold the station in 1983. Cochran had been the only manager who had managed to stay on with the new owners.

"Certainly Taft won't call him as a witness, and because he is out of the area, we can't subpeona him. But at least we have his deposition, and it is pretty damaging because he admits that you reported the harassment. He also admits to the fact that he took Cochran's advice when he made the decision to fire you." Louis was trying to convince me that Conshafter's absence wouldn't hurt my case. I didn't believe him.

"Remember, Cochran called Conshafter while he was in Chicago and told him you had gone to the luncheon. At least we can enter that testimony into the record," he said in an effort to soothe me. "And, don't forget, we have all the evidence you put together regarding your performance while you were an employee of Channel 2. That's going to help us a great deal in court."

Louis was referring to the evidence I had put together making, what I hoped, was a strong case for my employee performance. I had diligently tracked my sales performance against everyone else's I had worked with over the three years. I knew I only needed to show that my performance was as good as anyone else's in my department, and after literally three years of research, I had shown it. The task had involved assembling and analyzing data and finally bringing it together in one book of comparative charts and graphs that would clearly show that my performance equaled or bettered my coworkers'. In revealing that, I would also prove that I was not fired for a performance failure.

Sometimes I wondered what it was I actually needed to defend myself against in court. The entire process before the trial seemed so removed from the original dispute. I did know for certain that I needed to show that I had been harassed—and it was going to be tough because the only person who had witnessed my harassment by Cochran was my roommate from the Toronto convention, Andrea Brookman. But thanks to my oldest brother, Rich, Molly McCoy (who now worked at a station in Denver) was being flown in to testify that the harassment had happened to her, and Andrea was also being flown in from Philadelphia to testify that she had seen Cochran harass me at the Toronto convention.

Louis and I had also found a total of nine women, mostly from Channel 2, who had experienced various incidents of harassment by Cochran. But, unfortunately, those who still worked at Channel 2 were reluctant to testify. They were afraid to jeopardize their jobs. And, I couldn't fault them. It was certainly how I had lost mine.

At the trial, I thought it was going to be pretty cut and dried regarding the reason the station had said they fired me. Because Jim Conshafter had admitted that he had made the decision to fire me based upon Tom Cochran's direct information regarding the Wilson luncheon, I reasoned that it would be fairly simple for the Judge to decide whether he thought it was a pretextual reason.

Conshafter and Cochran had both said in their depositions that I had been fired for attending the anti-drug luncheon. Because I was sure it was a pretty flimsy reason for dismissal, I was equally confident the judge would recognize this excuse as nothing more than a desperate attempt to get me out of the station to cover up a badly handled sexual harassment situation.

So what was really bothering me was the sudden flood of countless reasons for my being fired that were being mentioned in all the pretrial paperwork that was prepared and supplied by Taft. Cochran had produced a clump of papers that listed all my errors as an account executive. He wrote about my failures in writing and placing orders properly, my failure to make budgets on certain months, and my involvement in too many community activities.

And according to the Taft attorneys, one of Cochran's close friends, a media buyer, was going to testify that I had failed to handle her account properly during the week I was on leave of absence. The other client who was angry with me for not returning his calls during my forced leave was also going to testify.

I was stunned that both of these clients were going to go into a courtroom and speak out against me. I was particularly surprised at media buyer, Maria Tucker. Other than her long time friendship with Cochran, I couldn't imagine what would motivate her to testify against me. She was one of three people at a struggling little advertising agency. In fact she had been the receptionist when I had first met her a few years before. I had been someone who had encouraged her to learn more about the business so that she could get more recognition with her company.

The other witness was a boisterous bulky man from a warehouse store located outside of Buffalo. The retail outlet sold gas grills and swimming pools at warehouse prices and aired commercials that used to light up the station's switchboard with complaints. During the commercials, a man would scream reduced prices at the top of his lungs while 35mm slides of the various products would streak across the screen, and all the while price tags would be flashing below like neon lights. At the end of one commercial, the spokesperson dramatically fell into the pool. The commercials were tasteless to many people, but because they usually ran late at night, viewer complaints were held to a minimum. Every time I told Jim Conshafter about a viewer complaint, he would grumble about how much he would like to drop the outlet as a client.

Channel 2 was the only station in Buffalo that would allow the commercials from Recreational Warehouse to air. The other three stations in town either wouldn't allow them on the air—or had already thrown them off the air.

After I had received word that Recreational Warehouse was going to testify against me, I also received a call from an account executive from one of the other television stations.

"I thought you should know that there is a strong possibility that Recreational Warehouse has a nice deal with Channel 2. They are suddenly getting great treatment as a client—good placement of their spots, prime time, anything they want. As I understand it, testifying against you is the reason why they are getting such preferential treatment. In fact, they've never had it so good."

I was upset, but I still thought the judge would see through whatever it was they were going to say about me, although I had no idea what they could say. Other than not returning their calls the week I was out, they certainly couldn't say I didn't service them. They never returned my calls. They were always so late in paying their bills with our station that several times Jim Conshafter had told me to tell them we just wouldn't run them anymore. They were always in trouble with our station so I knew they couldn't say anything about client service. I personally had borne the brunt of their late payments. The commission from their outstanding bills was deducted from my paycheck, so I usually gave their account special attention.

Recreational Warehouse was my least dependable or respectable account. In fact, when I first started at Channel 2, I was given the account jokingly by Jim Conshafter, because he said no one else at the station wanted it. He called it the rookie account but somehow it had remained with me. So I was pretty sure Recreational Warehouse's testimony wouldn't be given much credence. The judge would probably not look favorably on a local merchant trying to get preferred advertising placement at the expense of a woman's sexual harassment trial.

December 1984

The "Godsend" in my life, at that time, came in the form of one magnificent performing arts center called Shea's Buffalo Theater. I had left the radio station and assumed the almost hopeless responsibility of trying to market a deeply in-debt theater, back onto its feet. Helping to keep life pumped into the major historic theater became a labor of love for me and gave me a wonderful and purposeful diversion from the seeming senselessness of the pretrial period of the case.

Shea's Buffalo Theater was the anchor of the theater district in Buffalo. In its younger days, Shea's had on its stage the greatest artists in the entertainment world. But in recent years, due to financial problems and a variety of political complications, the theater was having a difficult time in both presenting shows and realizing any profit.

When I arrived at the theater, a new director was in place, along with some very ambitious and risky programming plans for the new season. The challenge of turning artistic opera, ballet and drama programs into box office winners was a huge undertaking, especially when the theater had no budget to promote such a full-scale program. Early in the season, the director and the board of directors admitted to their basic differences, and I was immediately named to act as director for the simple reason that I possessed experience in performing arts marketing and because there was no one else who could quickly take over the top position quickly. My own years of performing on stage and my experience in directing and producing came in handy. I understood artists and the language of theater so I was comfortable working with stage managers, agents, and touring companies. My years of broadcast and retail advertising and sales promotion had more than taught me everything I needed to know about promoting shows. Although my paycheck was still small, I had more than a job, now; I had a mission. The staff of people I worked with were dedicated and tireless and other than experiencing a few standard initiation tests to see whether I knew my stuff, they didn't seem to be concerned that they were working for the first woman director of Shea's Buffalo. Like my position at Channel 2, once again, I had unwittingly landed in another job where I was the first woman ever to hold the position.

Although my work at Shea's gave me great purpose, the trial was still hanging over me like a thundercloud, and I knew the board of directors undoubtedly was feeling a little squeamish about my extracurricular legal activities. I was still working at Joe's law firm preparing evidence for the trial on Saturdays and Sundays, and often fell asleep at night with the latest pretrial papers in my hand. Although I tried very hard to keep my exact daily involvement in the lawsuit quiet, I doubted that I was very successful at it. As I already knew, sexual harassment lawsuits are pretty hard to sweep under the rug.

Finally, in that winter of 1984, the seventh trial date was set for December 10.

This time it looked as though it was really going to happen. Seven days before the trial, an attempt was made by the court's magistrate to settle the case. Once before, there had been a settlement conference held where Joe had reported back to me that Taft seemed to be interested in offering us $70,000 to keep it out of court. But within days, Joe regrettably informed me that they had pulled back on the offer, and were only willing to offer $30,000. And Joe knew that $30,000 wouldn't even begin to cover his legal fees. The issue of settlement was dropped.

It was hard to believe that finally the circumstances which had occurred while I worked at Channel 2 were going to be presented to someone in authority. I had high hopes about the justice system and even higher hopes about the judge who would be presiding. The judge assigned to my case had earned the reputation of being one of the most liberal judges in the country. Chief Justice John T. Curtin was going to hear the case.

With the trial just days away, it was still hard for me to

believe that I—who had always been so concerned about what other people thought of me, and never wanted anyone else to be angry or upset with me—was now headed into federal court to bring action against my former employer, a multimillion-dollar corporation. It wasn't as though I was going up against the corner store. The family name of Taft is easily found in the pages of American political history. Taft Broadcasting owned Hanna-Barbera Productions, "Entertainment Tonight," television and radio stations, and amusement parks.

On the other hand, because of the dramatic change in my compensation since I had left Channel 2, and because of the lawsuit, itself, my savings were now completely gone. I suppose those on the other side of my lawsuit thought I had some nerve taking them on in court. But with or without the financial clout my opponents had, I believed that I had the facts on my side, and from the bottom of my heart, I also believed they would be enough to win.

Chapter 7

Plaintiff on Trial

"Call the first witness," said the King; and the White Rabbit blew three blasts on the trumpet, and called out "First Witness!"
"Give your evidence," said the King, "And don't be nervous, or I'll have you executed on the spot."

Alice's Adventures in Wonderland
Lewis Carroll

"Joe, *he* shouldn't be in the courtroom, right now—should he?" I was leaning over, whispering to Joe, and referring to Cochran. I had become alarmed when I noticed him seated near the back of the courtroom as the opening statements had concluded and the direct questioning was about to get under way. As I heard my name being called as the first witness, I got up from the plaintiff's table and made my way around to the front of the table, stopping abruptly in front of Joe when I realized that Cochran was in the courtroom and would be able to hear all of my testimony.

"Joe?" I asked, almost in the form of an order that I sent sailing over my shoulder, as I made my way up to the witness stand. And as I was sworn in with my hand raised high, I gave Joe one more look that told him I wanted Cochran out of the courtroom. It wouldn't be fair, I thought, if he was allowed to sit through God only knew how many days of my testimony. It would give him ample time to study my testimony and an unfair advantage in preparing his own rebuttal to my statements.

I sat down in the witness chair and took a deep breath. How ironic, I thought as my stomach began to churn, to be in a positon now that was going to require my best efforts to maintain total and complete composure. It would be the maximum stress test of grace under pressure, and I wondered silently if I would be able to pass. No matter what happened in this courtroom in the days to come, I would have to refrain from reacting to anything said—or done. With this trial finally happening—after three long years of strife—it would be very difficult not to show some sort of emotion during the unavoidable painful moments and memories of just how all of this needless nightmare began.

As I smoothed out the straight skirt of my neutral-colored-and-appropriate-for-trial suit, I couldn't help but remember the words I had used in training students in stage competition regarding the importance of appearing graceful even under tremendous pressure. Now, as I adjusted the microphone before me, I was putting my own theories of poise to a hard-core endurance test in a setting that would surely appall any respectable debutante. Even as I sat there waiting for the questioning to begin, I couldn't believe that my problem at work had thrust me into the role of witness. But as I tried to shake off the sudden feeling of bewilderment that probably comes with the first day of any trial, I comforted myself with the assurance that soon this unpleasant mess would be over. After all, at last we were finally getting down to business. We were now in front of a chief justice of the United States District Court.

The courtroom looked just as I thought it would. The wooden walls of the grand room seemed to rise up endlessly to points too lofty to easily see. The judge's bench was centered at one end of the courtroom and appeared solemn and imposing like a sacred altar. With or without the judge seated behind it, its noble structure and dimensions would be humbling to anyone who stood before it.

The pungent scent that filled the space of the massive chamber was a pleasing mixture of the rich and spicy fragrances of leather and wood. Yet, there was something more in the air that seemed to stir the senses. It was a presence you couldn't see or smell—it was something you could only feel. Maybe it is what the legal scholars term "justice" or perhaps it is the pure sensation of contest, the rush of contention and debate found so exhilarating by the masters of litigation—but something more powerful than the mere anticipation of drama overtook the stately room in which we were gathered.

I believed in the room. Everything around me looked and smelled like justice, so I decided I must trust it. Oddly enough, though, the only thing that didn't seem to fit in was the judge, himself. He was small and elfin with twinkling blue eyes set in the handsome face of a man who looked like he enjoyed life. His ever-so-slightly wrinkled shirt peeked out from underneath his black robe and spoke of his apparent lack of need to impress the inhabitants of his courtroom with a showy display of costume or airs. His gray hair was slightly tousled, showing his also seeming disregard for the label "distinguished." The judge appeared to be a regular guy—a nice man, no booming and fearsome Wizard of Oz—yet probably someone who shouldn't be underestimated. I had researched some of his earlier court decisions regarding some deeply controversial issues, and I knew he was unafraid to interpret the law strongly and boldly. Perhaps his most famous decision, regarding Buffalo Public School desegregation and busing already had proven that he was undaunted by public opinion.

Joe approached the bench and the judge slowly and rather reluctantly acknowledged his presence. Joe asked—for the sake of a fair trial—if, at his honor's request, the courtroom could please be cleared of other witnesses who would be testifying in the case.

With eyebrows raised, the judge slowly glanced around as though he were giving Joe's request some thought. After a moment he agreed with Joe that all of the other witnesses should leave the courtroom at once. His eyes widened slightly when he watched only one man rise at his request. The judge's eyes narrowed as he watched Tom Cochran go over to Frank Stewart, Taft's lead attorney, whisper something, then turn to go. As Cochran unwillingly left the courtroom, Judge Curtin watched him walk down the aisle, past the guard, and through the double doors to the outside hall. His eyes remained on the doors long after they had closed behind Cochran.

At that point, I was pretty sure that Judge Curtin was doing a first-glance study of both the defendant and the plaintiff in this case of sexual harassment. The judge yawned slightly as he settled back in his chair, and with a casual motion of his hand, he asked Joe to begin his direct line of questioning.

My first day of testimony was both long and tiring. I also wasn't able to get much sleep the night before because the threatening phone calls came steadily throughout the night like the last frantic hour of a telethon. I recognized that it had been ridiculous of me not to turn my phone off. But, for some stubborn reason, I would not react in such a logical manner. The telephoned death threats that had come over the past three years had become a contest of stamina between my unknown tormentor and me. I was not going to give in during the final hour.

Instead, I had longed for a sound night's sleep, but reasoned that I probably wouldn't have slept well, anyway, considering that I had to begin testifying the next morning.

I remained on the witness stand the entire first day, and although I was concentrating fully on my testimony, I couldn't help but notice the judge who sat before me. His constant fidgeting was going to take some getting use to, I thought, but what was really worrying me was the judge's open and clear hostility toward my attorney. Something wasn't right between them.

Before the second day of court opened, Frank Stewart approached our table and asked if he could discuss a serious problem with Joe. The two attorneys met in front of the judge's empty bench and spoke earnestly for several minutes. Frank Stewart's face was clouded and Joe appeared to be deeply concerned and rather moved by what he was hearing. The only words I was able to overhear were those of Joe's. "That's terrible—how upsetting," Joe remarked somberly. The discussion lasted for several more minutes until Frank Stewart pulled off his glasses, shook his head for a final time, and walked back to his own table.

Joe took his seat next to Louis. "What was that all

about?" I whispered across the table to Joe. I was concerned. Obviously something terrible had happened.

"Apparently Cochran received an anonymous threat last night. I guess he's pretty shaken up about it. So is Frank. Frank was concerned that it was too much for Cochran to handle during the trial." Joe was now looking down at his notes and already lost in his own thoughts.

My mouth dropped open. Because the trial had generated a lot of press in the past few weeks, it was obvious that someone had read the story, didn't like what he was reading, and decided to give Cochran a call. I started to speak, but Louis grabbed my arm. "Forget it," he said, "I know what you are going to say—just forget it."

Louis knew what I was thinking. This trial was about harassment, specifically sexual harassment. Taft Broadcasting's defense regarding my claim of sexual harassment was to minimize the offense; treat it as a minor and insignificant misunderstanding rather than a series of threatening and frightening offensive acts. Yet, today, Frank Stewart was gravely alarmed that one anonymous call to Cochran during the week of the the trial might be too much for his client.

Louis didn't respond when I asked him offhandedly whether I should give Frank Stewart the name of the police lieutenant who had helped me through my three-year ordeal of threatening telephone calls. "I could be a big help to Stewart right now," I said lightly, "I know all about dealing with harassment."

Louis continued to ignore me. He was disgusted, too, but knew that it was pointless for me to be upset about what I had just heard. And, of course, he was right. We had more pressing matters before us.

The second day of testimony proved easier than the first. Joe seemed much calmer, although Judge Curtin continued to show great hostility toward him. After court that day, I asked Joe if he ever had a previous row or conflict with Judge Curtin. "Was there any reason for him to be so hostile?" I probed, as we walked back to Joe's office. "No," said Joe to both Louis and me, for Louis seemed quietly concerned as well. "I think he just doesn't like the case," said Joe, very matter of factly, "but you are right; it's pretty clear he's not happy about something."

On the third day of my testimony, Frank Stewart, the lead counsel representing Taft Broadcasting and its employee, Tom Cochran, circled me in the witness stand, moving like a jaguar sizing up his prey. His outward style and mannerisms oozed southern gentlemanly charm, but his demeanor cloaked determined resolve to bring me to my knees. Frank Stewart was fully aware of the purpose of his mission in Buffalo. By electing to handle Taft's defense in my case, it was his goal as a trial attorney—as it was the goal of the multimillion-dollar company he represented—to win. By not allowing me to prevail in my claim against Taft, Frank Stewart almost singlehandedly would slow down—if not completely stop, other employees in the company from even thinking about suing Taft for such things as sexual harassment. Not only would winning this case be a personal coup for Frank Stewart, it also would firmly seal the floodgates of discriminatory action claims that could be brought in the future by any other wronged Taft employees. For him, winning the case would assure his client of tight control when it came to addressing employee disputes. If won, the case would be a cost-effective manner of keeping a lock on discrimination suits. The task before him was a stimulating challenge for the southern lawyer, and he seemed to be relishing his deputation.

Being questioned by Frank Stewart was like participating in a well choreographed fencing match. While maintaining an effortless air of easiness, he crossed and checked swords with me until he thought he detected a slight tear or weakness in my testimony. At those moments, he would lunge forward quickly and artfully, stabbing at whatever I had said with a sharp and piercing motion. I had to be on my guard constantly. It was a keen game of mental alertness, and we continued to duel across all the territory that had been covered before, during my three days of examination before trial. Although it was without question the most stress-filled experience of my life, I clung to the thought that everything I was going through now was taking me closer to the moment when it would all be over.

During the direct questioning, Tom Brydges, the first person I had gone to long ago regarding my problem with Tom Cochran, also served as a witness and testified to the fact that I had asked him for advice regarding the harassment the very day it started to happen. The judge knew Brydges, and for the first time in several days seemed to perk up. Laugh lines appeared on his face and I thought I heard him chuckle softly when Tom Brydges said that, because he represented corporations in litigation, he normally appeared in the courtroom "on the other side."

Hearing Curtin laugh was reassuring. In a humorless case, it was nice to know that the judge had a sense of humor. I was sure that Tom Brydges' testimony had helped my case. It was apparent that Judge Curtin was listening to him.

An expert witness and CPA, Dan O'Connell also testified as to the authenticity of the charts and graphs that were displayed on an easel near Curtin's bench. O'Connell verified that my performance as an account executive was as good as, if not better than, that of my coworkers. The testimony of the burly Irishman also seemed to hold Judge Curtin's attention.

But for the rest of the first week of trial, the judge did not seem to be particularly interested in Joe's efforts to get to the heart of the issue. During Joe's examination of Cochran, the judge seemed to be in another world entirely. While Joe slowly and methodically picked apart and examined each and every one of Cochran's alleged complaints regarding my performance, Judge Curtin continued to get in and out of his chair restlessly. The hours ticked on, and the judge seemed to be getting farther and farther away from the matter at hand. He stretched and yawned. And more times than it seemed appropriate, he stopped Joe in the middle of a sentence and asked him what his point was going to be—or if, in fact, he had one at all.

I sensed we had completely lost the judge's attention when we literally lost sight of the judge, himself. Because I was busily writing down testimony so that we could review it that evening, I had been listening intently to Cochran's answers to Joe's questions when Louis poked my arm and asked me, "Where the hell is Curtin?"

Louis was right. The judge was not in his chair.

Curtin was gone from the bench and completely out of sight. I knew he had to be somewhere in the courtroom but swiveling around in our seats, neither Louis nor I could spot him anywhere. Finally he stepped out from behind a large blackboard that had been pushed aside in the far lefthand corner of the courtroom. He had been behind there for at least ten minutes, maybe even longer. Louis and I wouldn't look at each other for fear it would bring on the kind of emotionally charged laughter that erupts when something seems funny at an extremely inappropriate time. Besides, I really had nothing to laugh about at this point. Judge Curtin was obviously not interested in hearing this part of the record, even though it mattered greatly to my case. I had waited three years for Judge Curtin to hear my case and now he wasn't even listening.

That night, I asked Joe why he wasn't focusing more on Cochran's behavior—nothing besides my own testimony was being introduced into the record about the nature of harassment. The main discussion seemed to stay centered on complaints Cochran had about me—and all of those complaints came after I was fired.

The trial was not turning out at all as I had expected. Sexual harassment was no longer the main point of the trial, in spite of the fact that it had been my only original complaint against Cochran. A fundamental problem had been buried beneath an avalanche of testimony. Lost within all the verbiage was the one reason I was in court in the first place. No one could convince me that I was the plaintiff at this trial because I was spending all of my time in court defending myself—and everything I had ever done or thought, or possibly failed to do, for that matter.

The trial clearly was zeroing in on me. Opened wide for all to see were all of my medical records since childhood. My personnel files from all my previous jobs were subpoenaed and carried to the front of the courtroom. My family doctor, John Argue, was asked if my father's death was to blame for any stress I might have been feeling regarding my claim of harassment. My extracurricular activities—past and present—were discussed as though they were espionage missions instead of just plain and simple altruistic interests I had pursued in order to give my life more meaning and depth.

The defense attorneys even took the time to bring to the court's attention enlarged professional photos of the desk and chair I had occupied at Channel 2. Carrying needless and absurd details of my life even further, the earlier record also included testimony, from another account executive, that I had brought homemade baked goods into the office on a regular basis. In fact, the account executive had said, I baked so much he wondered when I had time to sleep. I cringed when I heard that remark, although I don't know why. Why should I be embarrassed that I happen to love baking?

The picture of my private and professional life was being painted by a group of legal artists who were succeeding in creating nothing more than a splotched and messy interpretation of my character, experiences, and abilities. The end result did not seem to resemble me—it was parts of me—but not all of me. Baking brownies, doing charity work, producing shows, a history of dancing and modeling lessons—Taft evidently was trying to make me sound like a sweet and shallow thing—complete with hoop skirt. In different words, they were saying I somehow had fallen from the apple tree swing into a job in the corporate world, and was now unhappy because the boys were kissing me and making me cry. A "Georgie Porgie" problem, your honor, not a corporate problem, they seemed to be saying. This young lady is getting in the way of business. Stewart had opened his trial remarks by announcing to the judge that "the plaintiff is certainly a charming lady BUT. . ." It disturbed me that they were taking my feminine traits and interests and using them to detract from the main issue.

My biggest concern was that the judge was being exposed to all this garble about "the plaintiff" and not hearing—or learning—anything about the actual act or nature of the harassment. I wanted him to understand how such treatment felt to someone who had experienced it; I wanted him to realize how it affected a person's job; I wanted him to comprehend what a powerful grip Cochran had over me when I worked for him under those conditions. None of that was coming out.

I asked Joe why nothing was surfacing about the type of person Cochran was, nothing was being said, by either side, regarding his behavior. Not a word was spoken about his personal life or his attitudes toward women. Only once, and very carefully, was he asked about the way he had forced himself on both Molly McCoy and me. No one, particularly my own attorney, was daring to cross the invisible line that was drawn around Cochran which seemed to be protecting him from the heartless scrutiny I was facing.

"I just don't think its a good strategy to expose Cochran in that fashion," Joe reasoned. "We are going to have Molly McCoy testify that he harassed her, too, and that should be enough. Our main burden of proof is to show that he had no other reason to fire you—or rather Conshafter had no other reason to fire you. We are going to prove that all of those complaints he wrote down after you were fired were just pretext. And we are going to show that they were minor if, in fact, they even existed at all. It's got to be obvious to the judge that Cochran, in a panic, went through your old files after you were gone, and tried to come up with a list of errors. By methodically going through each of Cochran's complaints, I think I'm effectively showing to the court that Taft is merely trying to bolster the record with evidence that was never a part of their original decision to fire you. That's all we need to prove, I feel. I'm sorry, but I just don't think we should get into anything more. And, I don't think we should attack Cochran, personally."

I thought Joe was dead wrong on this specific aspect of

our strategy. How would Judge Curtin know about the type of person who harasses women on the job if he wasn't given any evidence or information that would enlighten him on such behavior? I didn't want Joe to attack Cochran personally but I did want him to bring out the harassment aspect of the case in a compelling manner. We were now into the second week of the trial, and I still felt as though the whole thrust of the trial had been lost in the parade of complaints regarding clerical errors that the defense wanted to show might possibly be connected to me in some way. Although those errors were never an issue during my employment at Channel 2, and had never been brought to my attention by management, they suddenly had become major points in a case I had instigated to raise the complaint of harassment.

Thankfully, Curtin put his glasses on top of his head and finally spoke out on the aspect of errors. At this particular point, the judge was starting to get very cranky about the business of television advertising. Feeling obvious exasperation, he spoke: "There are literally, I trust," he said moving his arms up and down like a pump, "it seems that every time you have a spot run on the air, there are many documents, and then for every day, there are many, many more documents. A week, I suppose could produce perhaps thousands of documents. Now, there is no burden on any witness to come in here and expect to recall what is in any document."

Joe moved on to asking Cochran the big question. Had he ever harassed me? Cochran calmly stated no. Had he touched me? Never, said Cochran. Had he ever kissed me? No. Joe's questioning of Cochran reached a quick and sudden dead end and we were close to ending direct testimony. I was horrified—was that all there was to it?

Momentarily, it would be Frank Stewart's opportunity

to call witnesses and I was sure his carefully chosen and groomed witnesses would have nothing good to say about me.

One of the first witnesses to appear for the defense was the media buyer, Maria Tucker. Stewart offered her a wide ear-to-ear smile as she hesitantly took the stand. He kept smiling and nodding encouragingly to her as she wiggled about on the witness chair in a effort to get comfortable. I found myself remembering back to when Cochran, himself, had told the story about the time he had aired the wrong commercial during an entire flight for one of Maria's two clients. He told us how sweet and understanding Maria had been about it. He had rolled his eyes and laughed about it. It was one of his favorite war stories. While I studied Maria, I tried to remember when that was—it had been sometime before I had taken over the account. But I guess it didn't matter, now. She was here and she was on the stand. Probably at Maria's request, Stewart began his questioning by over-emphasizing the fact that she had been subpoenaed. He first asked her to tell the court why she had been dissatisfied with my performance as her account executive. Soon it was obvious that Maria's main complaint was that I had not placed one important spot in a televised Buffalo Bills football game in the first week of November—the same week I had been sent out of the station on a forced leave of absence. Maria said she thought she had ordered the spot just about three days before the game. She said it was a last minute buy. When the spot did not run in the game, Maria couldn't reach me so she called Cochran and complained to him about my performance, and asked that I be removed from the account. When cross-examined by Joe, Maria said that she was not aware nor was she made aware, by Cochran, that I had been placed on a forced leave after receiving the order for the football game. Although I was out of the station on an unscheduled leave of absence that was not of my own choosing, an outside client, Maria Tucker, was never aware of the internal crisis going on within the television station that had failed to run her spot. All she knew was that her client's spot had not run. The "spot" she was referring to was one of the orders that had remained on my desk when I had been asked by Conshafter to leave the building immediately.

I could hardly wait to hear what the guy from Recreational Warehouse had to say about me.

Gary Doebler took the stand with more zeal than I thought a witness should reveal. He seemed to be truly excited about spending his day in federal court instead of remaining back at his warehouse to sell pools.

His story was astounding. He never stumbled once and it poured out of him as water might rush out of one of his famous discount plastic pools if it were to suffer from a large sudden puncture. I listened with disbelief as he expounded about his months of dissatisfaction with my service. He hardly took a breath in his tale except to smile broadly when the judge commented that he and his wife had seen Doebler's ads on television and "were always meaning to take a drive out to the warehouse for a better look at his discount gas grills."

Doebler beamed and continued on with his story. Joe threw me a dirty look that told me he was angry that I had not prepared him for this damaging testimony. I couldn't have forewarned Joe about the story we were hearing, for I had never heard it before today.

"It's made up, Joe—all of it. I told you someone warned me that Channel 2 had an arrangement with him."

When Joe cross-examined Doebler he succeeded in bringing out the fact that Recreational Warehouse had indeed—either been banned from the other television stations in town or had not been allowed to advertise on them at all. Joe then asked Doebler what he paid per television spot on Channel 2.

"We get an excellent rate," boasted Doebler. "We pay $50 per spot and we're even in prime time." Joe asked him if he was aware that the prime time cost of advertising was between $500 and $2,000 per television spot. Doebler said he knew that—that was why he thought he got a great rate at Channel 2. "TV is the lifeblood of our business," said Doebler rather smugly.

It sure is, I thought, as I watched him leave the witness stand. And it seemed apparent to me that he would do anything to keep that blood flowing.

That night I had to appear at a dinner where I was to receive an award presented by the National Organization of Women—the "Women Helping Women" award. I was not a member of the local chapter but someone in the organization had been following my long, drawn out plight and had nominated me for the award. Right now I felt as though I wasn't helping any woman—especially myself. Both Maria's and Doebler's testimonies had been tough to take. And earlier that day, Sue Pearce and Dino's testimony hadn't done me much good, either.

Ironically, the guest speaker at the dinner who offered the general remarks on my award was Sheila Murphy, the former anchorwoman from Channel 2 that had since run for local office and won. It had been three years, earlier, on the same day as her fundraiser, that Cochran's behavior began to change the course of my life. She told the audience that all who were present that evening needed to remember that I was not the one on trial down in federal court this week and that my efforts would help all women. When I accepted the award, I had little to say except that I was doing the best that I could, "down there" in federal court. But inside, I was upset about what had happened in court earlier and I was starting to get nervous about being at the dinner too long. Under the category of "when it rains, it pours," my transmission had gone on my car earlier in the week while driving to court one morning, and I now needed to pick it up before the garage closed. I had also told Joe and Louis that I would meet them at their office after I stopped in at the dinner. At the close of court, today, both of their faces had looked grim. I knew our meeting tonight would not be a good one.

It was eight o'clock p.m. before I arrived back at Joe's office. Joe looked beaten, and obviously believed that he was. He had little, if nothing to say. Louis and I carefully reviewed our notes readied for the rebuttal that would take place during the final day of testimony. We had lined up several area media buyers who would testify that my performance as an account executive was good. I was also going to get back on the stand and testify that everything Doebler had said was false. I also wanted Joe to put the impartial investigator, Sue Pearce back on the stand, and ask her if she had ever done any sort of investigation before, and, if in fact, she had ever received any training to conduct such an investigation. I was sure the answer to those questions was no, and I thought the court should be aware of those facts. As far as I was concerned, the internal investigation had just been a cover-up and I wanted Curtin to know it.

Louis had to leave to keep an appointment with Ralfa Musialowski, one of the witnesses who would be testifying the next day. Joe and I were left alone.

"We've lost, kiddo. It's over," said Joe, defeatedly. "Doebler's testimony was just too damaging."

I was sure Joe was going to cry at that moment, otherwise I think I might have. But my reason for feeling on the verge of tears was because my lawyer was telling me he had given up and we still had one more important day in court.

"Joe, he lied," I stressed. "Can't we overcome that tomorrow? Put me on the stand for as long as you need to—I think it will help." I wanted to beg Joe not to give up. I had come too far to have my lawyer declare defeat even before the trial had ended. I had heard that Joe had received tremendous pressure from his partners regarding this particular lawsuit. It wasn't going to be the money-maker it had once been thought to be, and through the grapevine I had heard that he had been asked to focus his efforts on cases that had the potential for greater profit. Joe was fairly new with his firm, and like any new law partner, he was concerned about his standing. I understood the position he had been in throughout the litigation and realized it was for that reason that I didn't get too upset when he had begun to distance himself from my case, a few years before. I knew the case was probably not as important to Joe as it was to me. But at this moment, I couldn't allow him to quit. We had another day in court and I needed my lawyer more than ever.

"I want you to know I think you are a really nice person," he said quite emotionally, "and I'm sorry that you are not going to win this case. I am deeply, deeply sorry," said my lawyer of three years.

I left Joe's office and went home to call the other witnesses to see if they had any questions about the next day's procedures. Alone in my apartment, I tried not to panic. If Joe was giving up, then it was critical that I did not. I called the witnesses who were to testify the next day and asked if they had any questions about the procedure. I was overwhelmed by their sincere interest in helping me. All of them were taking time off from work to testify in my behalf. Their willingness to help me touched me deeply and helped to offset the terrible feeling I had been left with after hearing Maria Tucker testify against me earlier in the day. At midnight Louis called and outlined what the order of the witnesses would be. If he had given up, too, he didn't let me know it, and I was grateful for that.

"Louis, one more thing," I said as he was about to hang up. "Tell me, again, why Andrea Brookman isn't at this trial. She was an eye witness and was more than willing to testify. How come Joe wasn't concerned that her schedule prohibited her from being here this week?"

Louis hedged my question a little bit by saying that it was just bad luck that my trial was being held during the Christmas season and that it was unfortunate that Andrea had to be in Florida with her family. It was almost one o'clock in the morning and I was exhausted, so I decided I wouldn't debate with Louis any longer on what was now a seemingly dead issue. But I was going to talk to Joe about it in the morning, whether he wanted to hear it from me, again or not. I had received numerous notes from Andrea saying she would be more than willing to testify—in fact, she had discussed it with her husband—and felt as though it was her responsibility to testify. She had remained concerned and proven to be a very caring person. She was a bright and articulate woman who would have been a key witness. We should have made it possible for her to be at the trial.

Joe seemed better the next morning and we found that some of his fighting spirit had returned. I gave him the questions that I had written out for his last interrrogation of Sue Pearce and I also handed him the questions I wanted him to ask me when I took the stand for the final time. As planned, I was to be the last witness called.

The series of rebuttal witnesses went smoothly. The five witnesses representing my major clients who were called to the stand, said in their own words, that I was a good account executive and had always provided them with good or excellent service. More clients than I could hope for were standing out in the hall ready to testify. One witness was missing his company's Christmas party, another was keeping a customer waiting, one media director was geting hives but they, and many more, had come forth to counter the negative testimony that had been given by the defense's two witnesses on the day before. Judge Curtin finally halted the stream of people that stood ready to take the stand by stating that he already knew what they were going to say and that there was no need for further testimony.

I was the last witness to testify and Judge Curtin called one more brief recess before I took the stand. Earlier, at my insistent and nagging request, Joe had asked the judge if Andrea Brookman could possibly testify after the holiday recess. As expected, Judge Curtin turned him down flat. "You've had all the time in the world to depose witnesses," he stated to Joe. "I'm not giving you any more time." Joe told the judge that the reason for his failure to depose such a key witness earlier had been shortage of funds. The judge came back hard with a double meaning remark that Joe did not want to hear. "These cases seem to generate a great deal of media attention for the lawyers handling them, don't they, counselor?" Joe's firm was one of the largest and most profitable firms in Buffalo. The judge knew full well that if his firm wanted to depose a witness they could.

The judge's later remark, was by all rights, a low blow. I hated to admit it, but the judge's first point was well taken. We had known about an eyewitness for three years and yet we had failed to produce a formal statement from her. We deserved Judge Curtin's remark.

Joe, Louis and I huddled together to discuss my final testimony outside the courtroom, and just as everyone was filing back into the courtroom, I excused myself to the ladies room. When I came out, the big, echoing hall of the federal building was empty except for Cochran, who was seated on a long bench opposite the door of the courtroom. Nervously, I noticed the courtroom doors were closed. Even the guard had already stepped inside. As I got closer to him, like a rabbit, Cochran proceeded to violently stamp his one foot down, moving it faster and faster—almost as though he wished to break right through the marble floor. The closer I got to the courtroom door, the more rapidly he pounded. His strange behavior was something I didn't want to witness alone. Feeling a little panicked, I picked up my pace and hurriedly pushed one door of the courtroom open. The judge was just returning from his chambers and was heading toward the bench. I caught my breath and collected myself. What had just happened outside the courtroom was weird, I thought. But this entire ordeal in court had been strange. I quietly walked to the front of the courtroom and took the stand. I was glad that within an hour it would all be over.

I stepped down from the witness box when Curtin nodded that it was okay for me to go. Joe seemed more encouraged about our final day in court and told me so as I joined him at the plaintiff's table. He mentioned a couple of things we should definitely include in our posttrial brief.

A few minutes later, anxious to get out of the courtroom, I moved out into the hall to speak to my mother, my younger brother, Tim, and a few of my friends. This had been the only day of the trial that my mother had witnessed. I really had not been too keen on having my mother see too much of the trial. I knew the final day of the trial would not be as rough as the previous days had been, so I had told her it would be okay for her to be there for rebuttal. During the entire trial, only one member of my family had attended. Each day, my brother Tim had quietly slipped into the back row of the courtroom. I assumed he had kept the rest of my four brothers—Bill, Rich, and Jim—apprised of the daily activities in the courtroom. I also assumed that his reports to the rest of the family were not particularly optimistic.

While I was standing in the hall, Frank Stewart tentatively came up to me and shook my hand. "Miss Neville, this has been the most difficult trial I have ever been through," he told me. With one good look him at him, I believed him. "I hope you understand that I was just doing my job." He paused and studied my face, "It wasn't anything personal."

"It was the most difficult trial I've been through, too," I said flatly, although my tired remark had been intended to be lighthearted. I said good-bye and wished him a Merry Christmas. It was obvious he couldn't wait to get out of Buffalo and head home.

Both looking wiped-out and drained, Joe and Louis also approached me to say good-bye. Louis was a newlywed and was headed to Albany to spend the holidays with his wife. Joe told me he and his wife were on an early morning plane to Florida the next day. He was exhausted, he said, and desperately needed to get away. While on vacation, he would make some notes for the brief, he told me. Just as Stewart had mentioned, Joe also confided in me that the trial had been hard on him.

I noticed that it was already evening when I walked out

of the court building onto the street. The last day of the trial had been so consuming, I had lost all sense of time. The icy frozen snow on the sidewalk was crunching loudly under me but the snow that was falling to the ground was gentle and silent. The golden-colored garland Christmas decorations tacked up upon the poles that lined downtown Buffalo's Niagara Square were swaying softly in the December night. The cold air felt good.

The trial was over. In a couple of days, it would be Christmas.

Chapter 8

787 Days Later

"What are they doing?" whispered Alice to the Gryphon.
"They're putting down their names," the Gryphon whispered in reply, "for fear they should forget them before the end of the trial."

Alice's Adventures in Wonderland
Lewis Carroll

Louis left the firm immediately following the trial.

That left me with no one to write the posttrial findings of fact and conclusions of law. The task was up for grabs in Joe's law firm and it soon became obvious that no one wanted the job. Finally, Joe informed me that Thea Lango, a new associate was going to work on the posttrial papers.

By that time, due to nervous energy and the secret fear that I might have to write my own brief, I had already pulled most of the testimony out of the transcript that I thought would probably be needed for the findings of fact.

I felt sorry for both Thea and myself. She was the fourth different lawyer assigned to my case, and I didn't know if I could stand telling all the hundreds of details of my story over again—to still another person. But if it was difficult for me, it was just as wearisome for her. Although perhaps one of the smartest women I had ever met, she hadn't even been at the trial and now she was stuck writing a brief for a case that looked to her, at first glance, like a real loser. During all the weeks we worked together on the brief, she continued to tell me not to get my hopes up. "Judge Curtin's record for deciding these cases in favor of plaintiffs is not good," she said. "In fact, sexual harassment cases in front of any federal judge do not, as a rule, fare well." She was also careful to mention that she believed Judge Curtin hated to interfere with a company making "in house" business decisions.

Thea and I spent a lot of time in strong debate regarding the treatment of sexual harassment cases by the courts. I argued with her that Judge Curtin had a big family, and, in fact, some of his daughters were close to my age. With daughters out there struggling in the working world, he undoubtedly would be sensitive to my case.

Very soon I figured out that Thea wasn't listening to me when I went on in defense of the fairness of the litigation process. Finally, I simply decided to believe I had succeeded in convincing her of this particular judge's level of sensitivity when I relayed to her a story about the time, years ago—while I was still working at Channel 2—that I had met Judge Curtin's daughter, Anne.

His daughter and I were both scheduled speakers at a career day held at a local high school in Buffalo. Judge Curtin's daughter was speaking for 20 minutes on a career in the FBI and I was speaking for the same amount of time on the opportunities available for a career in the field of broadcasting. In fact, I told Thea, the event took place at noon—just like the Wilson High event.

Judge Curtin's daughter and I had been introduced to each other by the head of recruitment for the FBI. I had come to know the recruiter because, while I was working at Channel 2, he had tried to recruit me.

The reason why I later remembered that it was probably the judge's daughter whom I had met that day was because the recruitment director had teased me by saying I was speaking on behalf of the wrong career field. He said I could have been speaking with Anne, instead. I had saved the program from the seminar and had noticed later that the name of the pretty woman who had spoken on behalf of the FBI was Anne Curtin.

I wanted to convince Thea that I was right and she was wrong. Certainly with a daughter like Anne in a predominantly male workplace setting, Judge Curtin would be sensitive to my analogous situation.

But Thea would never comment. On those occasions, she would mention softly that she thought I might find myself being disappointed by the inability of "the system" to satisfy every disagreement in a courtroom setting.

So, I felt as if I had won a philosophical war when, after we finally finished the brief, I noticed that Thea had become noticeably more enthusiastic about the case. One day, out of the blue, she confided in me that she truly believed that I had done the right thing in fighting back. She had joined me in being hopeful about the outcome. She said that all we could do now was wait for the decision.

After the final summation was over and the brief was filed, we expected to hear from Judge Curtin within a few months. At the close of the trial, he had reassured both sides that he would try to make a quick decision. He told us on the final day of trial that he knew how important the decision would be to all of us.

TWO YEARS LATER

Months passed and there was no word from Judge Curtin. Not only was I anxious about the decision, but I also was becoming worried about the delay itself.

After two years had passed since the trial and there was still no sign of a decision from Judge Curtin, I began to speculate wildly about why the judge kept putting my case at the bottom of his pile. I wondered if perhaps I was being punished for daring to bring my matter to the court's attention. I knew that the federal judge was busy, but there just seemed to be no excuse for such a long and painful delay in a matter that should have received the judge's attention months earlier.

I became convinced that Judge John T. Curtin was never going to make a decision. I felt he was going to let the clock run out on my case—or worse—on my life. I had heard of age discrimination claimants actually dying before they made it through the final stages of the court system. "Maybe that was what was going to happen to me," I bleakly told my mother one day.

Since the trial, I had made the difficult decision to leave my position at Shea's Buffalo Theater. Although I loved the work I had been doing, I felt as though I no longer wanted to handle all the necessary stress and strain of running a huge performing arts theater. Much to my dismay, I was feeling exhausted physically; apparently the trial had taken a lot out of me. I thought that perhaps a less stressful job would be a good idea while I awaited the outcome of the trial. Once the trial was behind me, I knew I would need all my energy to get my career back on track.

My days at Shea's Theater had provided the perfect opportunity for me to make a local "comeback." I believed my work at Shea's had been a positive step in redeeming my career. My performance record at Shea's had freed me from the stigma of incompetence that had attached itself to me when Channel 2 had fired me in 1981.

I also felt disheartened when I became aware of cutting remarks one of the young male members of the board of directors had been saying about me, and after going through the trial, I was in no mood to tolerate any additional personal attacks. I was crushed when I overheard the young board member talking about me prior to a meeting where I was scheduled to give the annual budget report. "When she hands you the report, make sure you don't touch her hand—she'll nail you for sexual harassment," the local business owner said. He continued to make jokes about my case, not realizing that I could hear him clearly talking in the conference room before I entered it. At the time, his insensitivity had both angered and disappointed me.

I was also pretty discouraged that my salary as the managing director was still about $20,000 less than the man I had stepped in to replace. I knew when I took the job that I had no bargaining power when it came to negotiating my pay, but now that the trial was over, I was anxious to start making a better salary again. After I announced my resignation, I wasn't surprised to hear that the man who succeeded me, although he had no prior experience in theater management, was offered a salary that was $26,000 more than mine. Just as the lawsuit was a constant reminder to me of the importance of fair treatment of employees, my current position reminded me further that when it came to pay equity for women on the job, there was some squaring-up that still needed to take place.

When the news that I was leaving Shea's was in the morning paper, a reporter from Channel 2 immediately called and asked for an interview. Because the reporter was not a Buffalonian, he had not been at the station or in the area when my suit had first been filed. He was either unaware or unconcerned that he was about to do a flattering piece on the woman who had been fired for "poor performance" by the station for which he worked. The theater was part of his beat, and he had frequently called me for straight stories regarding the turmoil Shea's had been experiencing, particularly in its lobbying efforts for local city funding. Now, in this news story, he was matter-of-factly offering me the credit for my significant role in bailing out and stabilizing the theater that was so dear to many people in Buffalo. He interviewed me on the 6 p.m. news and stated that it was good marketing that had helped steady Shea's Buffalo Theater during a troubled time. I found it rather ironic that Channel 2 had aired a story on the competency of someone they had not only fired, but had even had to testify in court to prove that they were quite justified in making that decision.

I left the pressures of the theater behind—and took what I thought was a low-profile marketing position for a real estate company—hoping I would start to feel better physically. I ended up landing in the hospital, anyway. While there I was forced to endure the scolding delivered by a well-meaning doctor. Having been active and fit all of my life, I had always taken great pride in my physical endurance and I was terribly upset that I wasn't the picture of health I liked to think of myself as being. Initially, I had only gone to the doctor because I thought I had a killer of a flu, but he had immediately put me in a hospital to spend a few days in a cardiac ward "to reconsider" how much stress I wanted to put myself through during the rest of my life.

I felt like nothing was going right in my life and, in fact, it wasn't. There hadn't seemed to be anything normal about my existence since I had first raised the issue of sexual harassment. For the months that it took me to return to a healthy physical state, I wondered if I had become ill because I was just so weary of waiting for the decision.

But what bothered me as much as any physical ailment was that everywhere I went someone would ask me whether the case had been decided. Even other judges in town were becoming more than just curious as to why I hadn't received a decision. One judge mentioned to me, in fatherly fashion, that I needed to get my lawyer to push a decision out of Curtin. "This is off-the-record you understand, but it's gone on too long," he said seriously, "Curtin can't make a good decision if he can't remember who the plaintiff is or what took place during the trial. Push your attorney. Do it. You need to get on with your life."

I begged Joe to press Curtin but he was still hesitant. He didn't want to upset Curtin, he told me. He was afraid that if he aggravated the judge, the ruling would not be in our favor.

November 1986

In total frustration, believing that the decision would never come, I decided it would be better for my well-being if I left the Buffalo area.

Hoping that a move would help put the circumstances of the case behind me and help me get on with my life, I relocated to Washington D.C.

Once I had made the difficult decision to move, I put

my plan into motion quickly. Within two weeks, I had found a public relations job at a tiny advertising agency in Georgetown. Although the job wasn't what I wanted, and offered no long-term possibilities, I was content enough with my decision to get a new start. At least I would be in a bigger city when the decision was handed down, and then I could start rebuilding my career.

Once in Washington, I began to offer counseling to women who were experiencing sexual harassment on the job. This time I wasn't counseling young women on getting into the right careers. Now I was trying to help women of all ages hold onto the jobs they already had. And with Capitol Hill within earshot, I found that there were many people in Washington who recognized the seriousness of the problem of sexual harassment. With such groups as the Women's Legal Defense Fund and the Congressional Caucus for Women's Issues headquartered in the nation's capital, it was reassuring to find many others who were also deeply concerned about the workplace issue that had been mostly responsible for my need to find a new hometown.

February 1987

It was during the third year following the trial that Thea called me and told me to come home. Believe it or not, she had said over the phone, the judge was finally going to release a decision. Although Thea had left the law firm, she still took it upon herself to stay close to the case; the case which looked like it might finally be coming to an end.

I immediately flew to Buffalo. At ten o'clock in the morning, an anxious Joe headed over to the federal clerk's office to pick up the decision. Thea stayed behind and waited with me. We sat in the lobby of the law firm and numbly watched the receptionist take the incoming calls and the elevator door open.

I thought I heard a clock ticking somewhere, but realized I couldn't be hearing one because there wasn't one in sight. Once again, I knew I was scared to death. The last time I had felt this frightened was the day I had gone into Dino's office to tell him I wasn't going to stand for my boss harassing me while I was working. I thought that day in Dino's office was the scary moment of truth. Little did I know then that it would be six years before the real moment of truth came.

In a few minutes I would find out whether Judge Curtin was returning to me my right to say no to sexual harassment on the job. That was what this fight was all about, and regardless of all the legal motions and briefs and testimony, that was the one simple question that needed to be answered.

There was really nothing else Judge Curtin could do for me except answer that question. A favorable decision would not return me to my role as a valued employee of Channel 2. It would not give me back the lost years. It would not take away the gossip, and the whispers, and the stigma of being "the sexual harassment lady"—as some had called me. No one probably knew how much I hated the unpleasant sound of the word "harassment." It didn't matter how many times I heard it mentioned, it still made my skin crawl. It seemed foreign—it didn't belong in my life.

As I sat waiting, one thing I knew for sure was that even a good decision would not make me forget. Over the past few years I had tried very hard to suppress some of the terrible memories I had about my experience. Because I couldn't seem to lock away all the darker days, I tried, instead, to reassure myself that something positive had come out of them. I found myself repeating that overused expression, "You are a better person because of all of this." But whether I liked such an expression or not, there did seem to be some truth to it. My experience had taught me some important lessons about life—Real life. Some of those tough lessons were learned while I was in the unemployment line or while I was searching for new jobs. Some were legal lessons. Many were about people and human behavior. They were hard lessons—painful lessons—but I had learned from them.

But the most important aspect of today's decision was that it wasn't just going to be mine. I was going to share it. I knew that my case wasn't only about my own circumstances, it represented literally thousands of women who are forced to face sexual harassment on the job every day but, for a variety of reasons, can't pursue any form of relief. I knew that a favorable decision in my case would likely set a precedent for many cases to follow and would help enforce the law that sexual harassment is illegal. I prayed that Judge Curtin had done the right thing. One way or another, this decision was going to matter.

The receptionist told Thea that she had a phone call and she left the room to take it. I sensed that something was wrong when I saw her face when she returned, but she offered no explanation. She tried to make small talk but I knew she was upset about something. She took her foot and flipped up the Persian rug on the floor. "Look, Neville, this is the reason why I left private practice. There is *no* marble under the rug," she said solemnly as she pulled the rug up as high as she could without attracting the attention of the preoccupied receptionist.

I let her divert my attention from the unsettling final moments of the six-year wait, and I, too, studied the subflooring of the area under the elegant rug. Although marble flooring trimmed the outside dimensions of the massive reception area of the law firm, there was no marble flooring under the rug. The interior designer had faked the appearance of a solid marble floor. "I told you not to believe in everything you see," Thea said as she stared at me intently. I knew what she was getting at—she was telling me again not to believe in the system.

Ten minutes later, the elevator doors opened. Joe had returned. "You lost," he said angrily to me as he charged past us and headed to his office. Thea and I just sat there for a moment before we both silently decided to follow Joe. By the time we got to his office door, he had thrown the decision on top of his desk and was dropping himself into his chair.

"You lost," he said again, all the while avoiding my expressionless stare. What he was telling me was crushing me. At that moment, I couldn't respond.

Thea, Joe, and I sat in his office for several minutes without saying anything. A phone call broke the silence in his office. A newspaper reporter was on the line, said Joe's secretary, and wanted to speak to Joe about the decision. He refused the call.

Joe picked up the decision and I realized that he was about to begin reading it out loud. His disappointment at what he held within his fingers was evident. He touched the pages in front of him as little as possible.

I grabbed the arms of my chair and braced myself for what I was about to hear. Even before he started reading, my mind began racing as I thought about how I would be able to accept the decision that had not gone my way. Joe had 40 pages of the judge's thoughts in front of him. I had lost, I thought sinkingly. I had been stupid to believe that it was going to turn out otherwise. Joe seemed to wait several more minutes before he cleared his throat and began to read the decision that had taken more than 787 days to make.

The first several pages of the decision described the business of televison advertising. Those were obviously just background. Joe scanned the pages of the decision until he came to the more relevant statements regarding the case.

"Defendants concede that the plaintiff's performance was satisfactory prior to April 1, 1981." While Joe read, I silently began to editorialize. Sure it was satisfactory up until then, I thought defiantly, for it was April 1981 when Cochran had become my boss.

"Plaintiff received a sales award from Taft for billing more than one half million dollars for the fiscal year ending March 31, 1981," read Joe. "She was given an enthusiastic evaluation by Mr. Conshafter on March 1981. In fact, in February of 1981, when a competitor, Channel 7, offered Ms. Neville a job at a higher salary than she received at WGR-TV2, Dinovitz and Conshafter urged her to stay. Defendants maintain, however, that plaintiff's work performance deteriorated after that point. . ."

Joe read on regarding the reason for my actual firing. The judge believed that Conshafter had fired me for attending the Wilson High event.

"The parties are in agreement as to the law of this case," Joe was reading very slowly now. "Plaintiff has the burden of proof in a Title VII action. He cites *McDonnell Douglas Corp* v. *Green*," added Joe, as he continued reading the decision. "She must make out a prima facie case of discrimination. Defendants may rebut this case by pointing to legitimate, nondiscriminatory reasons for the action to take place against her. To prevail, plaintiff must then show, by a preponderence of the evidence, that the reasons given are pretextual, or that discrimination was a determining factor in the discharge."

Thea had a sickened look on her face and was shaking her head. Her pained appearance she showed, matched the same sensation I was feeling in my own stomach.

Joe stopped reading for a moment, giving me more time to think about what I had just heard. This decision seemed to be saying that, even though I was successful in proving that harassment took place, I had to prove also that I was a perfect person while on the job otherwise the company could fire me for anything that fell under the loose term of "a legitimate reason." I suddenly wondered if the court was saying that it was okay to harass people sexually who weren't the "superstars" within the organizational structure of a company. At the time I was fired I was Career Woman of the Year, had just received a sales award, and had never had less than a glowing performance review. It had been a piece of cake for Taft to fire me when I had complained of harassment. If proving you were harassed on the job wasn't enough—according to Judge Curtin—what was enough? Did you also have to be completely flawless? My God, I thought, all these years, and the wrong standard of law might now be being applied. Something was wrong with what I was hearing.

Joe looked up. "McDonnell Douglas," he said slowly and carefully, "McDonnell Douglas?" he repeated thoughtfully.

Thea echoed his words and turned to me, "Yes, McDonnell Douglas," and, with that, Thea leaned forward in her chair and began counting off the points of the McDonnell Douglas case with her fingers. She rapidly began to recite, "The time-honored test set forth by the Supreme Court in McDonnell Douglas," she stopped for a moment and looked intently at me to see whether I knew what she was getting at—and I did.

Once she thought she had my attention, she continued quickly, "According to that case" she emphasized, "a person must prove that he or she is a minority by race, sex, or ethnic heritage and that he or she was job qualified. The person also must show that he or she was fired or not hired or even not promoted—and finally—that the job slot was filled by a nonminority who held the same or lesser qualifications as the plaintiff."

"But," said Thea slowly, "as far as I know, this quote-unquote termination rule of law and test from McDonnell Douglas applies only in cases when a minority is fired or not promoted or not given tenure or a salary increase." She started to say more, but stopped.

In my mind, I finished what she was going to say. *But this test is completely irrelevant to a person—minority or not—who is sexually harassed on the job.* My head was filled with what I was thinking and what I was hearing. A sexual harassment victim can sometimes stay at her job—receive raises, get promoted—especially if she complies with quid pro quo favors. But that has nothing to do with the separate act of sexual harassment, I thought. That was what the 1986 Supreme Court case *Vinson* v. *Taylor* was all about. A victim should only have to prove that the sexual harassment was unwanted. I remembered, then, the first discussion Joe and I had had—years earlier—when he had explained to me what he thought were our trial objectives. He had said that he thought we must prove that Cochran had no real reason to fire me and that I was sexually harassed on the job. I thought about all those charts and graphs I had painstakingly produced to defend my work performance. But that wasn't what my case was about. My case wasn't about work performance—it was about sexual harassment. My professional pride had motivated me to get caught up in an effort that was not the most relevant issue. There was an aching feeling in my heart that we had tried the wrong case—from the start.

I realized Joe had begun reading, again.

Curtin's decision began to get into what the judge thought was my first burden as a plaintiff. Regarding the sexual harassment that had taken place in the car, the judge stated in his decision that he believed my testimony over Cochran's. He believed that sexual harassment had taken place. "While the fact that the plaintiff told a friend [Tom Brydges] about the incident does not establish that it occurred, it does refute suggestions made by defendants that Ms. Neville fabricated the story at a later time to avoid losing her job. Furthermore, plaintiff also reported the incident to Cochran's supervisior, James Conshafter, several days later."

The judge went on to say that I should have reported it to the next highest level of management, Dino Dinovitz, rather than Conshafter. The judge made reference to the company policy on sexual harassment that stated that the general manager of the station should be informed. The judge also noted that Jim Conshafter had apparently failed to notify Dinovitz. The judge did not take into account that I eventually did take my complaint to Dino after Conshafter hadn't acted upon it. Although this particular issue was evidently a technicality, obviously the judge wanted to slap my hand for not reporting it to Dino first.

Joe's face clouded when he went on to read the judge's next point. The judge stated that because all the instances of sexual harassment were not included in the EEOC complaint, he felt that they either didn't occur or that were unimportant and hadn't bothered me. The judge carefully mentioned that the EEOC complaint had been prepared with the assistance of counsel. I wanted to say something to Joe at that point, but I realized it didn't make any difference now. It was too late.

In concluding the section regarding sexual harassment, the judge stated that Cochran's physical actions toward me and his threat were sufficient to make out a prima facie case of quid pro quo sexual harassment prohibited by Title VII.

Joe was wide-eyed, "That was my entire case! I proved the sexual harassment took place—what made us lose then?"

Thea and I didn't respond, although we both had pretty much figured it out. Joe's answer came within the very next paragraph of the decision.

"While plaintiff offered some evidence that her performance was not consistently worse than the performance of other account executives, and that some clients were pleased with her service, I find that the reasons for her dismissal were not pretextual and were within her employer's discretion."

Instead of saying my performance was consistently as good as the other account executives, Curtin had said that my performance was not consistently worse than the others. Wording is everything, I thought.

Thea turned in her chair to face me. Her face told me that she was sorry that she had been right all along. It was the issue of legitimate business decisions and it was right here in Judge Curtin's decision as she thought it would be. I remembered the day she had told me that Judge Curtin did not like to interfere in business decisions.

The next several pages were almost identical to the posttrial brief that had been submitted by Taft. Pages and pages went on to talk about spots that had been missed and confusion about who was responsible for them not running properly. The judge also mentioned that there were some months that I hadn't made my budget, although my coworkers hadn't made their budgets either. He did mention that "other account executives also had difficulty reaching their budgets throughout the spring and summer of that year. While plaintiff's budget performance alone may not have been a factor, in combination with others, defendants were entitled to take this into consideration."

Next, the judge talked about the fact that the defendants had produced two clients who had complaints about my service. I rested my head on my hand when Joe began reading about the testimony given by Gary Doebler from Recreational Warehouse.

The judge had decided to believe his every word. The only thing said in my favor by the judge was that he noted that nothing was ever said about this client until the day I returned from my leave of absence and was fired. Joe read the judge's final remark on the testimony of Recreational Warehouse. The judge made a note that I disputed the legitimacy of any complaints from Recreational Warehouse.

The judge next covered the testimony of Maria Tucker. The fact that she had a complaint about my service the week I was on leave was taken by the court as a client complaint and it supported Cochran's testimony regarding my performance level.

I wanted Joe to stop reading the decision. I didn't want to hear anymore. But Joe kept reading, for now the judge was addressing the Wilson High event. Judge Curtin believed that this was the reason I had been fired. Although Jim Conshafter was not at the trial, the judge accepted the account given by Conshafter in his deposition.

The judge also felt that the internal investigation was done in good faith. He noted that it was not relevant to the case that Sue Pearce, the impartial internal investigator, had insisted on concluding her investigation that no sexual harassment had taken place. The judge also mentioned that I had failed to ask for Molly McCoy to be interviewed by Sue Pearce during the investigation. I stopped Joe. "Wait a minute—he's got to be kidding!" I was upset. "The judge expected *me* to know that Molly McCoy—in the newsroom—had been harassed by the same man who had harassed me? I didn't even know it had happened to her until after I was fired." Apparently Judge Curtin was telling me that, before I was even fired, I should have been responsible for tracking down all other employees who may have been harassed at Channel 2. Talk about a burden of proof. This is too much, I thought.

Joe started to continue, but stopped and looked sadly at Thea. "He doesn't even have Molly McCoy's testimony within the decision," he said numbly, "it's down at the bottom of the page as a footnote. She was a major witness at the trial—another employee of Channel 2 who was sexually harassed—and her testimony is only a footnote." Of course he has another victim of sexual harassment as a footnote, I thought dejectedly. Because of what was presented at trial, Judge Curtin had treated the case as a termination issue and not a sexual harassment one.

Joe looked down and read the final sentences of the written decision. Before his conclusion, the judge mentioned that although the telephone call placed by the community relations director of Channel 2 to L.L. Berger's could have been characterized as a retaliatory action, because of my good working relationship with Berger's, I was not injured as a result of the call.

Curtin's last words in the decision were no surprise to

me and they certainly did not surprise Thea. Joe read the final paragraphs slowly and carefully:

"After careful consideration of all the evidence, I find that the plaintiff was dismissed for legitimate business reasons. . .however even if plaintiff's performance was as good as that of other executives, the errors and client complaints provided a basis for her dismissal. The question is not whether the court would have fired plaintiff, but whether defendent was acting within the bounds of its legitimate business judgment."

A case about termination all put neatly into a package and tied with a bow. Where was the case on sexual harassment? I wanted to leave Joe's office immediately.

I was glad when Joe told us he had a luncheon appointment with a client. I had to get out of the law office. I was completely stunned by what I had heard. The six years of the lawsuit had been a complete waste of valuable years of my life. I had come up empty.

But it was more than my personal anguish that was bothering me; I was dwelling on the standard of judgment. Morally, the decision seemed wrong. What troubled me most was that the very reason for the lawsuit was belittled by the steady stream of irrelevant facts about my termination and work performance. Instead of following the directives of Title VII law, designed to protect employees from sexual harassment, Judge Curtin had somehow mistakenly viewed the "harm" in my case as being the termination, itself. Obviously thanks to the way we had presented the case to Curtin, the judge had missed the point. The "harm" and the actionable wrong in my case was the harassment all by itself. It was for this, alone, that Taft should have been liable. Without this logical result, I thought, any employee can be sexually harassed, offended, molested, or assaulted and no employer would ever be liable unless—and until—he later improperly fired that sexual harassment victim. Had the decision in my case produced a legal setback in the law? Had I succeeded in making things worse for future victims? I had to talk to Thea.

At lunch I asked Thea if she thought I was crazy to appeal the decision. She said she thought I was probably out of my mind, but mentioned that she might be, too, because she was thinking the same thing. She told me she knew of a terrific attorney in New York City who might take the case. The lawyer she had in mind was experienced in Title VII cases. But she was quick to caution me that an appeal would only be as good as the testimony of the district trial. No new evidence can be presented—I'd have to work with what I had.

After lunch, as Thea and I were about to part, she mentioned to me that Joe had called her from the court clerk's office after he had picked up the decision. He had wanted Thea to tell me that I had lost the case so that he didn't have to break the shattering news to me. Instead of delivering his message, she had pointed out the absence of the marble flooring in the reception area. In her own way, I guess she had delivered Joe's message, after all.

That night, huddled in bed, I tried to accept my loss. Losing the case was a bitter pill to swallow, but I knew myself well enough to know that I could get beyond the fact that things hadn't gone my way. I knew that it was just another legal decision—I had to keep things in their proper perspective. I thought about the day when one of my dearest friends from college had found out that she had multiple sclerosis. To this day she quietly fights it and never complains. And another one of my closest friends had lost her only sister in a senseless car crash that had occurred the week before I had been fired at Channel 2. In comparison, losing my job, my nest egg and my case seemed much less significant as compared to what life threw in the paths of others.

But, I thought, as I tried to fall asleep, the question of whether women have the important right to say no to sexual harassment had not really been answered—it had been buried by Taft's defense and all but ignored by Judge Curtin. I still needed an answer and I knew where I was going to go to get it. I honestly didn't know how I was going to get through another battle in the court of appeals. But, for some strange reason, I simply wasn't through believing in the legal system—just yet.

Being idealistic was becoming an expensive fault for me, I thought, as I began to figure out how I could possibly afford an appeal.

PART TWO:

THE NEW SEXUAL RULES FOR MEN AND WOMEN ON THE JOB

What happened in my case, shouldn't have happened at all.

If I had known the best ways to report sexual harassment on the job, it is very likely that this story would have ended the day I first walked into management to report it. In fact, had Tom Cochran followed the rules that managers must follow regarding sexual harassment, rules issued by Channel 2 to all employees, it is more than likely I wouldn't have had to make any report about his behavior at all.

If our manager, Jim Conshafter, had known enough to notify the General Manager of the television station as soon as he had heard me raise the complaint of harassment, together they could have consulted the company's legal counsel and probably found quick and painless solutions to an in-house personnel problem.

All it would have cost Taft Broadcasting was a phone call. Instead it cost all of us more than $500,000 and seven years.

Both employees and employers must be aware of—and follow—the simple and easy-to-understand rules regarding sexual/social behavior on the job. Because, when these rules aren't followed, the results often develop into an expensive, senseless story that isn't very pretty for any of the unfortunate individuals who find themselves involved. A story, in fact, that is much like mine.

These are the rules experience taught me. I hope they keep your workplace safe.

The New Sexual Rule for Men and Women on the Job

1. Trust your instincts.

When you suspect a fellow employee's intentions are of a sexual nature, don't wait for trouble to develop. Do something immediately to discourage that behavior.

2. Know your working environment.

Pornographic or suggestive literature, sexual jokes, demeaning remarks, and sexual antics should not be permitted. If they are, your working environment is ripe for sexual harassment.

3. Know whom you work for—and with.

Pay attention to the behavior patterns of your colleagues. If you know, for instance, that someone in your workplace is openly having an extramarital affair outside the office, there's a good chance he or she could be looking for one inside the office. How colleagues treat others, is a good indication of how they will treat you.

4. Know the rules.

If your place of employment doesn't give you their official policy regarding sexual harassment, ask for it.

5. Know your own comfort level, and

6. Know the comfort level of others.

Fellow employees will not suspect they are being sexually

harassed, if they have been treated with personal respect and concern from the beginning. If you firmly establish yourself as a concerned human being, your working relationships will be comfortable and productive.

7. Know your priorities.

Work comes first in the workplace. Meeting, dating, and even marrying someone you meet through work are possible, but not on company time.

8. Establish clear boundaries.

If you won't date fellow workers, let them know. If you will date coworkers, know the rules and follow them.

9. Learn to let others know how you feel.

If you or someone you know is being sexually harassed on the job, confide in someone else at work. And by all means, let the person who is harassing you know how you feel about it.

10. Know when—and how—to speak up.

Know your company's policy about the time, place, and way in which you should report social/sexual behavior that is interfering with your work.

Chapter 9

The Signs of Harassment

Shame versus Blame

Coming forward with a complaint can be a daunting ordeal to someone who has been sexually harassed. "Ninety-five percent of all women and men who report sexual harassment fear retaliation and a loss of privacy," says Mary Rowe, Ph.D. Special Assistant to the President of MIT. "They also feel it is pointless to complain—management won't do anything."

"Sexual Harassment in the Fortune 500"
Working Woman,
December 1988

RULE NUMBER ONE: TRUST YOUR INSTINCTS

The signs of harassment were there for me, right from the beginning. At first, it was just an uncomfortable feeling, nothing I could really put my finger on. It was so subtle. In the beginning, I would have had considerable trouble articulating to someone else what was actually taking place. It's much like the description people try to give others when they have sensed they are being followed or stalked on a busy street. You can feel someone else's intentions. Outwardly everything appears normal. But for some reason, you know it is not. Little kids often refer to this sensation as "the creeps" and now, so do I. My boss's first-stage behavior gave me the creeps.

Right then and there, I should have known that my instincts were trying to warn me of some sort of potential danger that could affect my job and my well being—danger that required some sort of action on my part. But like most people, I was focusing all my energy on career advances not sexual advances. And, besides, I was not a likely candidate for sexual harassment (or so I thought.) I was educated and I was a professional. I had executive status within the company. According to the station manager, Dino Dinovitz, I was on the inside track for many future promotions within the corporation. And, finally, I thought that everyone in the company knew my own personal set of rules. I was no one to fool around with at work, or anyplace else, for that matter. Without being particularly obvious and certainly without appearing righteous, when it came to important moral issues—if the right opportunity arose—I would quietly let others know where I stood. If anything, I was probably viewed by others as perhaps being a little "too straight." I thought that if someone at work was going to look around for someone to have an affair with, he wouldn't come near me.

When it came to even anticipating something like sexual harassment, I couldn't imagine it happening. It just sounded so tacky and it seemed likely only if there were partial, if not complete, willingness on the part of both parties. No, sexual harassment was something that happened only in the "Beetle Bailey" cartoon strip regarding the boss's never-ending pursuit of his secretary, Miss Buxley.

I had barely noticed the Taft company policy on sexual harassment that came stapled to one of my commission checks one day. I kept it, as I did all other company interoffice mail, but I didn't give it more than a glance. But that was before I became a target for my boss's advances.

Basic Misconceptions

There are many common misconceptions in the working world about sexual harassment. Before the media recently got hold of the statistics regarding its strong and destructive presence in the workplace, no one really knew the extent or seriousness of the problem. When those startling figures became front-page news stories and features on national talk shows, people began to acknowledge its existence in various forms. When individuals began reading that in isolated workplaces, up to 94 percent of their females admitted to being sexually harassed while on the job, and that widespread statistics show that one in every three women on the job say that they have been sexually harassed, the seriousness and extent of the problem finally was acknowledged.

But sexual harassment in the workplace is hardly a new problem. In fact, it is merely an old problem that has finally gotten the attention of management, media, and the general public. Although people are now noting that something called sexual harassment exists, it still faces a great deal of contention.

Prior to my own experience with sexual harassment, I had definite misconceptions about the topic. After my experience, when I began to counsel others, I was not surprised to find that my own original misconceptions about the issue were shared by a majority of men and women. First, I discovered that no one was able to come up with a definition of it or describe it easily. People would mutter under their breath that sexual harassment might have something to do with "pinching girls in the office."

Aside from the fact that merely mentioning sexual harassment to others is more than likely to raise eyebrows, I also found out that people are afraid and uncertain about sexual harassment, and, in fact, extremely reluctant to even talk about it. Many would much rather assume that it just doesn't exist in our sophisticated, people-oriented working world.

Although sexual harassment and rape are usually separate and different types of crimes (yet sexual harassment not dealt with immediately and properly has been known to lead to workplace rape) they share the same public stigma: It's dirty. Let's not talk about it.

By not pulling the issue of sexual harassment out of the corporate closet and discussing it as a professional and social problem, we continue to rely on many of the following common basic misconceptions:

1. Nice women don't get harassed.
2. Women ask for it.
3. Men don't get harassed.
4. Sexual harassment is only a blue-collar problem that happens when women take nontraditional jobs.
5. Sexual harassment happens only to promiscuous and willing women.

6. It's merely a crude form of socializing done by the uneducated.
7. Sexual harassment exists only in the minds of women who have overactive imaginations.
8. Sexual harassment is only an attention-getter for "old maid" types.
9. Only uptight and maladjusted women with sexual and social hang-ups claim to have been harassed.
10. Troublemakers use claims of harassment to retaliate against a supervisor or coworker.
11. People who are incompetent and fear the loss of their jobs hide under the "discrimination" umbrella and claim that they are being harassed in order to save a job they otherwise wouldn't be able to hold onto it.
12. The issue of sexual harassment is raised to mask a communication problem between a manager and a subordinate.

Later on, all of these basic misconceptions will be studied more closely, and clear and precise definitions will be given as to what is—and isn't—sexual harassment. But for now, suffice it to say that anyone who is courageous enough to raise the issue of sexual harassment has more to lose than to gain. It is more than likely that the person is telling the truth. Rarely are claims of harassment unfounded and without merit. According to the Fortune 500 report on sexual harassment, 64 percent of companies agreed that most complaints they receive are valid. As stated by one respondent, "more than 95 percent of our [employee] complaints have merit."

A Basic Definition

The basic, "no frills" definition of sexual harassment can be put into one simple word: unwanted. If someone has experienced an unwanted advance while on the job, then in that person's mind and private world, he or she has been sexually harassed, and no one—not judges, not attorneys, not company policies, not friends, not anyone else—can tell the victim differently.

RULE NUMBER 2: KNOW YOUR WORKING ENVIRONMENT

The first sign that may alert a working person to the potential or possibility of sexual harassment being permitted in a working environment may be found by studying the actual atmosphere of the workplace, itself. The following examples of workplace attitudes and behavior will alert you that your workplace is an environment where sexual harassment is already happening or more likely to take place.

1. Pornographic or suggestive literature, pinned up on bulletin boards, taped over someone's desk, hung in general work areas means anything can happen. This also includes cartoons of a suggestive nature displayed in working areas or distributed as interoffice mail. This could also include obscene chain letters. This is a clear sign that the company has a very permissive attitude toward sex. Don't think for one second that these "girlie shots" are only found in informal work environments like factories, gas stations, and construction site offices. Recently, a Wall Street firm found out that the women employees strongly objected to this sort of "interior decorating."

2. **Sexual jokes** or innuendo used during meetings or at staff functions. Beware if your manager freely tells off-color jokes or allows other employees to use professional time to tell such inappropriate jokes during meetings or gatherings. Humor in the workplace is great for relaxing people—and it often succeeds in making employees enjoy their work more. But crude jokes rarely make people feel at ease.

3. **Demeaning remarks** made regarding women or men in regard to their sexual identity. Keep in mind that men aren't the only ones who are making these remarks.

4. **Sexual emphasis.** Normal business conversation is sometimes twisted into meaning something of a sexual nature. Waitresses and service people probably bear the brunt of this, although people in all professions get hit with them.

5. **Sexual antics.** These so-called clever antics supposedly are done in the name of fun. However, they occur not only at the expense of the person the joke is on but at the expense of everyone in the office whose misfortune it is to be subjected to it. A few years ago, while working at a small public affairs firm in Washington, D.C., I was standing near the receptionist's desk when a woman walked in carrying a boom box instead of the expected briefcase. She was a stripper and had been hired to perform for one of the male vice presidents who was about to be married. The president of the firm and the other male vice presidents thought they had put together a terrific office gift. The consensus of the staff, including the "honored" VP, was that it was a tasteless and out-of-place act. It did not belong in the office.

7. **Quasi-prostitution: all in the name of business.** This sort of behavior is very common in the sales field. "Let's

send Stacia out to that client. He loves women." "Go ahead, Stacia, play up to him—show him our new line of equipment and show him yours at the same time."

What Signs Did I Ignore?

I vividly recall two incidents that should have alerted me to the type of environment I was working in at Channel 2. Because everyone dressed well, made an excellent salary, and was a respected professional in the communications field, I suppressed my own secret thoughts about my working environment. Remember, I was the first woman account executive and I kept telling myself that I should be thankful for just being there.

The First Sign

In 1979, during the second month of my new job at Channel 2, a jockstrap kept showing up on my desk in the morning. I would pick it up with my pencil, and matter-of-factly drop it into my wastebasket. The next day another one would magically appear on my desk. Finally, one morning, the usual piece of male sporting gear was conspicuously absent. Apparently, whoever was responsible for the daily presence of my very own personal reminder of the prevalence of males in my department, was no longer getting the desired response from me.

The Second Sign

This sign not only offended me, it hurt me, too. Even though I was the only woman of a seven-member team, I really thought I was accepted and respected by the men in my department. I found out otherwise in 1980 when it came time for our annual sales luncheon. At the end of each fiscal year, our department manager would host a luncheon for the team at one of the better restaurants in Buffalo. It was a good way to end one year and begin the next. Just minutes before we were supposed to leave for the luncheon, the sales secretary came into my office and told me that there was something I should know. Apparently "the guys" had gotten together and thought it would be "a real scream" to have the luncheon moved from the Park Lane restaurant to The Cobbler Shop. The Cobbler Shop was a seedy little bar that featured topless dancing as its noontime entertainment. Thanks to the sales secretary, I was able to avoid the luncheon treat. At noon, while "the guys" were smiling smugly and eagerly putting on their coats, I went into Jim Conshafter's office and told him that I was sorry, but a client had just called and needed some last-minute "availabilities." I felt terrible, I told him, but I really couldn't make the sales luncheon. I hoped he would understand.

The look on all of their faces when they returned from their tasteless luncheon told me that I had definitely ruined their day, and to top it off, their food was pretty lousy, too. The luncheon only would have been fun if they had been able to watch my face while I had to sit through the "costumeless choreography."

I received a flower arrangement at home that night. The note attached to the flowers told me it was from the management of Channel 2, thanking me for my hard work during the previous year. But the flowers didn't change the fact that Channel 2 had allowed such a tasteless prank to take place. I never forgot it, but, unfortunately, I didn't recognize it as an important indication of attitudes at Channel 2.

RULE NUMBER THREE: KNOW WHO YOU WORK FOR—AND WITH

Pay Attention to the Behavior Patterns of Others

If I had paid close attention to my boss's behavior patterns, I might have been able to prevent the sexual harassment I experienced, or at least I might have been able to deal with it without having to pay such a huge price. My boss's prior patterns of behavior clearly showed me that he was more than capable of using—and, furthermore, was definitely the type of person who would use—his position and power to harass a subordinate.

Without question, it is vital to your job security to know your own boss's behavior patterns. When you work closely with someone, it is usually possible to spot an unethical professional, but it is a lot harder to determine the exact rules by which a person lives. In order to be able to protect yourself from becoming innocently involved in someone else's encounters or romances, as well as to guard yourself against sexual harassment, you must be able to anticipate—not only what your boss may expect from you as an employee, but what eventually may be expected of you personally.

I am not suggesting that you preoccupy yourself with every move others around you make, but I am advising you to watch how they behave in certain situations. People establish behavior patterns in both their business and personal lives. If your boss is married and you happen to know that he or she is openly and comfortably partaking in extramarital affairs, it can be a signal to you that your supervisor is willing to break certain promises made to society and to others. If you are aware that our boss engages in unethical business practices, such as padding clients' bills, or lying to clients and customers you also can assume that he or she may be willing to break other kinds of professional rules. If your boss is not doing right by other people in his or her life, there is no sound indication that he or she won't break a rule at some point that involves you. I am not suggesting that if your boss breaks some rules, you may become a victim of sexual harassment. However, I am advising you that you should have a sense as to what type of person you work for—your superior's set of values and rules may not be ethical. And down the road, that may be a problem. Pay attention. How the people who make up management behave toward others will help you determine how they eventually may behave toward you.

A true tip-off

Chances are, if you work for—or with—someone who might be capable of harassment, someone else in the office may very well warn you about it if that person has reason to believe the potential for that sort of behavior exists. Sometimes a woman will warn you, but it might also be a man who's willing to tip you off. Ethical men find the practice of sexual harassment as horrifying as the women who experience it.

While I was doing a live call-in radio talk show in Philadelphia, an overwhelming number of calls came in from men who were concerned about the behavior of other men in their office. Many men don't like to see sexual harassment happen. If they can warn a woman about a culprit without jeopardizing their job or putting themselves in the middle of an office drama, they will tip you off. Listen to them closely when they share the information with you. They may only mention it to you once.

I received a tip-off very early in my employment at Channel 2, from Jim Conshafter, no less. But, because I wasn't expecting anything unpleasant ever to happen to me, I failed to pay any attention. It was around 6 p.m., and Jim, Tom Cochran, and I happened to be leaving the station at the same time. As we stood at the front door, we realized it was raining pretty hard. As usual, my umbrella was in my car. Although both Jim and Tom had umbrellas, Jim was more than quick in offering to share his. While Cochran walked through the rain in front of us, Conshafter offhandedly remarked to me, "Kath, good thing you are under this umbrella instead of that one."

"Why?" I asked, curious about his comment.

"You don't know about Tommy?" he said lightly and apparently without thinking. It was after I became interested in what he was saying that he suddenly changed his mind and decided to drop the subject. "Oh, never mind," he said quickly. "Have a nice night," he added as we got to my car and he went on to his. What he said that night meant very little to me at the time. But it certainly meant something to me, later.

Chapter 10

Definitions That Draw Lines

> *What complicates instances of subtle discrimination and harassment even more, says Kathleen Neville, is that their definition sometimes differs from one person to the next. "We all have a line," she says, "and if someone crosses that line, we make the personal decision that we've been violated professionally and personally, and we take necessary action."*
>
> *from "Breaking the Code"*
> *Savvy*
> June 1988

RULE NUMBER FOUR: KNOW THE OFFICIAL RULES

In today's working world, no one who goes to work can afford to go about his or her own daily business without being aware of what the "official" rules are on issues of sexual harassment, dating coworkers, and superior/subordinate relationships. Not only are the stakes too high regarding the future of your position if you should find that you've broken a company rule in the social/sexual arena, but, more important—if you find yourself in a dispute regarding your social/sexual behavior on the job, you could damage your entire career—greatly and permanently.

Those who have been fired because of incidents of sexual harassment or have fallen victim, in some way, to any other social/sexual relationship that may have been unearthed by coworkers or management, usually don't escape without reflections on their employment history.

And, if it's possible to feel an even worse impact beyond the effects such situations have upon future career plans—internal company disputes that later become legal disputes sometimes do irreparable damage to lives. Unfortunate individuals who don't learn about the proper social/sexual rules on the job sometimes find themselves learning all about them in courtrooms. Those who don't take definitions seriously—or don't feel the rules apply to them—find out the hard way. By ignoring definitions and breaking rules, they actually may change their careers and lives forever.

Off-sides and holding

Everyone understands the need for good sportsmanship when it comes to national pastimes such as football. The rules and regulations of the National Football League are universally understood. Players and spectators accept the importance of and need for those rules. It's part of what is known as playing fair. At crucial moments of a game, packed stadiums have been known to become bedlam when they witness a player breaking such rules as holding onto another player's facemask or jumping offsides.

A personal foul is recognized as an unfair practice in the

game of football. Just as those rules are designed to protect the overall goals of the game of football and the principles of good sportsmanship, so are the intentions of certain behavioral rules in the workplace. Not only do good working rules on the job help ensure that the workplace is a healthy one, they also allow individuals greater ease and comfort in meeting their job requirements. They promote fairness. And although they are more complicated than the basic rules surrounding good conduct in sports, they still help to achieve the same goals. If a person is being bothered by illegal sexual harassment or unfairly overlooked for a promotion because the supervisor is having an affair with a subordinate, the workplace is not showing proper corporate fair play. When one or more individuals breaks the social/sexual rules, there is simply nothing fair about it—for anyone.

Many employees have a difficult time understanding legal definitions of social and sexual behavior on the job. Not only is it difficult for them to understand how such a wide range of emotions and behavior patterns can even be put into legal terms, but the legal language—in itself—is confusing.

Individuals who may be skeptical about the actual need for rules and definitions regarding social/sexual behavior on the job, usually understand the basic and fundamental principle behind those rules when they begin to comprehend the importance of the necessity for workplace social/sexual "law and order."

It is largely undisputed that generally the dynamic of men and women working together is healthy. There is a positive and productive energy to a workplace that is made up of both sexes working together. The results of such teamwork shown by men and women who work and strive together compatibly is unmatchable.

Some employees believe that the need for rules and restrictions about social and sexual behavior on the job is just one more way to wrap their lives even tighter in restrictive red tape. Isn't it enough that our actual job responsibilities are tightly controlled, they say—is it really necessary for someone else to dictate to us just how to act and behave as a social and sexual being while on the job? According to many others, including most companies and the courts, the answer is yes.

Breaking and bending rules is out

Today, the general public seems to be extremely intolerant of those who break rules. The major media stories regarding the nation's high-ranking political figures, top company officials and even religious leaders are all about exactly who is breaking rules. And those rules include the social and sexual rules of people who have been unsuccessful in wiggling out of the spotlight lately. All the previously unspoken rules about what used to be safely stored and locked away in the area called "private lives" have been hauled out and exposed in the brutal light of day. Once out of the shadows, presidential candidate Gary Hart didn't have a chance of recovering from his social/sexual no-no.

The public seems to be demanding that the moral rules of law and order be followed by everyone in positions of responsibility, including those in the working world. And the public is making a good point. In order for companies to maintain corporate social law and order, and to further reduce their liablity on their own turf, they must establish rules and guidelines for their employees to follow. There are safety rules, environmental rules, operating rules, and, now, because the human resource make-up of the workplace has changed, social/sexual rules for all employees to follow.

No longer can employees brush-off a complaint of sexual harassment by saying they didn't know that they were breaking any rules. Ignorance of the rules is no longer an alibi. "I didn't know I was doing anything wrong" is no longer a sound or suitable defense.

From *Sexual Harassment*, a handbook offered by the Washington, D.C., law firm of Arent, Fox, Kintner, Plotkin & Kahn, this explanation of the Equal Employment Opportunity Commission guidelines on sexual harassment is offered:

> The EEOC (Equal Employment Opportunity Commission) guidelines define illegal sexual harassment as unwelcome sexual advances, requests for sexual favors, and other verbal or physical conduct of a sexual nature, when combined with any of the following facts:
>
> 1. Submission to the conduct is made a condition of employment. For example, if a female employee is told by a new boss that she will be fired if she does not sleep with him, she is a victim of sexual harassment.
> 2. Submission to or rejection of the conduct is made the basis for an employment decision. This situation might exist where, for example, a woman is told that she will get a raise if she sleeps with her boss, but will not get a raise if she refuses.
> 3. The conduct seriously affects an employee's work performance, or creates an intimidating, hostile, or offensive working environment. An example of this situation would be presented where a female's co-workers were constantly making jokes about her figure, and touching or grabbing her.

The EEOC first introduced these guidelines on sexual harassment in 1980—less than ten years ago—and only one year before my own entanglement with the rules of sexual harassment (see appendix). Within the past ten years, many companies have used these guidelines to develop and build their own policies regarding sexual harassment. Because the EEOC guidelines are generally followed by the courts when such cases appear before them—they are generally accepted as the universal rules on the issue of harassment.

In 1986, right in the midst of the middle-of-the-road Reagan era, an amazing thing happened regarding such things as the definition of sexual harassment and the liability of employers. Much to the astonishment of the working world, the U.S. Supreme Court spoke on the issue of sexual harassment in the workplace. In a surprising decision regarding *Vinson* versus *Taylor*, the conservative court ruled that a supervisor who sexually harasses a subordinate discriminates on the basis of sex and that Title VII forbids sexual harassment even if the injury is not economic in nature. (See appendix) The Court also said that for the harassment to be actionable it must be sufficiently severe or pervasive to alter the conditions of the victim's employment and/or create an abusive working environment. Further the Court noted that an employer might not be liable for a hostile environment if the company has a grievance procedure and a policy against harassment and if the complainant failed to invoke the procedure.

So now, even the Supreme Court realizes that rules need to be refined when it comes to the matter of men and women in the workplace. The highest court is acknowledging that social/sexual behavior on the job can be a major problem in the workplace to both employers and employees. And because the court did recognize its presence, its members felt the urgent need to issue more solid rules—and clarify old ones. The only problem with rules coming from the courts into the workplace is *how* these rules are introduced, interpreted and finally enforced within the work environment. Because, of course, such rules are only good when they are actually applied and practiced.

A primary lesson in sexual harassment

There are two main types of sexual harassment: *quid pro quo* (you give me this, I'll give you that) and *hostile work environment* (an intimidating, hostile, or offensive atmosphere). It is not always necessary that the employer or supervisor be specifically aware that he or she is inflicting one of these types of sexual harassment upon an employee. For example: Someone said to me once that he couldn't have possibly committed an act of quid pro quo sexual harassment because he didn't know what it meant. And even others have attempted to convince themselves that they are not guilty of contributing to a hostile work environment because they are very quiet and not at all hostile about the way they bother and annoy the same person day-after-day.

Once individuals understand what these two types of behaviors are, they must also understand all the different faces they may have in the workplace. Many specific types of acts fall between these two broad categories—and it is between those wide cracks that the confusion begins and remains.

A Closer Look at Definitions

To simplify what the EEOC guidelines are is to put the definition of sexual harassment in another way.

The Power Threat

Quid pro quo is all about using the power one individual has over another for the sake of personal gain or enjoyment. You simply can't ask a subordinate or coworker to sleep with you in order for him or her to receive a raise, or perk, get a promotion, or have better working conditions than other employees. Nor can you ask that person to sleep with you to avoid losing his/her job. That's a threat and a form of sexual blackmail.

The Polluter

Those individuals who help create a workplace environment that is unsuitable for other people to work in because such individuals are continually and repeatedly exposing others to sexual remarks, gestures, suggestive pictures or pornography are polluters of the workplace atmosphere and guilty of sexual harassment.

You can't bother others at work continously by saying or doing things of a sexual nature so that you annoy, upset, or offend them to the point of interfering with their job or the jobs of those around them. That's why this second type of sexual harassment is appropriately termed "hostile work environment"—because it causes great anxiety and ultimately a good deal of antagonism within the workplace environment. And people can't work effectively if they feel as though a "sexual war" is going on all around them. They certainly can't be productive if they happen to be targets of such abusive behavior.

Some Ground Rules

Because the two types of sexual harassment are general behavior patterns, there are specific kinds of behavior which should not take place in the workplace.

Inappropriate Remarks/Shades of Implication. You should not refer to a coworker or a subordinate as a sexual human being or refer to his/her physical looks in a sexual manner. Telling a coworker she has nice legs is out of place at work. Telling a coworker you had a dream about him last night is also out of place. Any thoughts of a sexual nature should be kept to yourself.

Sexual Generalizations/Sexual Put-downs. You should not make any insinuation that others at work are of less quality or ability because of their sex. Although the issue of discrimination has been discussed widely and is strongly discouraged in today's companies, it still is going on—and sometimes is coupled with shades of sexual harassment.

Terms of Endearment. Calling any coworker or subordinate such names as "cutie," "blondie," "honey," "dear," or "sweetie," should be avoided in the working environment. Sometimes they are harmless expressions of affection for a subordinate, but they are just not acceptable for addressing another employee. They are intimate terms, not workplace names.

By Any Other Name Is Just Not the Same. No nicknames for coworkers or subordinates that you or anyone else thought of—are allowed at work. Nicknames are acceptable only when an employee insists that you call him or her by his or her own chosen nickname and the self-chosen name is appropriate for the workplace.

Danger Zones and Out-of-Bound Compliments. You may tell someone how nice he or she looks—if you say exactly that. But if you dare to get creative or specific in your compliment, you may cross the border of good taste and sexual harassment. Remember that you need to be concerned with what the other individual's own personal definition of sexual harassment is. For example, if you tell someone else you like the way her dress fits rather than just complimenting her on how nice she looks, you are knowingly or unknowingly implying something to her. Keep your compliments general and sincere—and safe.

The Body Snatchers. These people are the body adjusters or the fashion police of the workplace. They pick at lint, adjust hair ornaments, snap men's suspenders, touch and pull on men's ties, play with jewelry, adjust belts, smooth shoulder pads, straighten hemlines, and generally touch other people at work. It is an invasion of the person being "pulled at and pawed" and can sometimes be very unwelcome. It's a kindergarten rule for sure, but keep your hands to yourself.

Corporate Kissing. The general rule in the workplace is NO KISSING. I disagree with those who loosely say that kissing at work is okay. Kissing is defined as a caress or a salutation. In the corporate world it can also mean either—and that is where the trouble starts. Unless your relationship with the person is an established and comfortable friendship that has been built and developed beyond and outside your professional relationship, I don't recommend kissing as a form of greeting a business associate. A good rule to follow is to ask yourself if the person you are leaning over to kiss gingerly is someone who has authority or power to alter or change any short or long-term aspects of your job.

Chances are, most people can get by just fine without kissing coworkers, clients, or bosses. Although some people believe it is very chic to spring a light kiss on someone before getting down to business, many others insist that it says a lot more about the person's genuine character, not to mention professionalism, when they don't kiss you hello but rather offer a warm and sincere handshake, instead of a kiss.

Rubbing Others the Wrong Way. These forms of physical contact don't really need any explanation. They simply don't belong in the workplace:

back rubbing
leg rubbing
knee touching
leaning
embracing
handholding
bumping or brushing up against another person

Guilty Eyes. Prolonged staring at a coworker or subordinate can be termed sexual harassment if it begins to interfere with the person's work. It is another nonverbal form of sexual harassment.

Dr. Heckle and Mr. Snide. Taunting and teasing another employee amounts to something called "heckling," which can easily amount to sexual harassment. "But I was just teasing" is the common defense of those who step over the line of friendly chiding. On the not-so-friendly side is the continuous act of delivering snide remarks to another employee that come in the form of "sexual snides." This type of behavior falls well within the category of hostile work environment.

Blaming it on Uncle Guido. One of the most common excuses for unacceptable behavior on the job is the one used by the person who insists that he or she can't stop his or her own behavior. "Hey, what can I say, it's in my blood. I'm Italian; we just naturally act this way." Blaming your behavior on your ethnic background probably would not please your ancestors or relatives in the least.

Sexual Harassment Outside the Workplace

Sexual harassment can and does take place outside the workplace. Often, someone harassing someone at work will continue to do it in other places and in other ways. Such behavior may include making unwanted visits to someone's home, calling the person repeatedly, sending the person letters—and sexually harassing the person while traveling together on business. Many victims of sexual harassment have told me about their discomfort and fear of being sexually harassed on a business trip.

Just because it doesn't happen in the office doesn't mean the offender isn't liable for his or her actions. It's still sexual harassment of another employee.

WHO'S HARASSING WHO—AND WHERE?

There is no stereotype when it comes to sexual harassment. Those who engage in it range from men and women suffering from serious mental illness to those who are merely unaware or culturally and socially ignorant of their inappropriate behavior. And harassers can take any form. They can be a line supervisor in a factory, CEOs of a Fortune 500 firm, artists, doctors, human resource specialists, accountants, film producers, repairmen, sales managers, lawyers, teachers, bankers or dispatchers. They can be extremely powerful and highly educated people or people without professional degrees, the person can be someone who is quiet or someone who is outgoing. The person could be married or single; rich or poor, good-looking or unattractive, well dressed or slovenly. It could be anyone.

And sexual harassment is found in large corporations, small businesses, factories, hospitals, human resource offices, government offices, military services, retail stores, art departments, shoe departments, law firms, real estate offices, construction sites, insurance offices, schools, television repair shops; in banks, network television offices; in coal mines, out on utility poles, inside operating rooms, on ships and in restaurants. It exists everywhere in the working world and no particular industry can claim that it is free of the behavior.

MOTIVATIONS

There are many different reasons why someone sexually harasses other human beings. Usually it is done for the sake of having power and control other another person—any person. Sometimes the reason a person practices sexual harassment is because they are reacting to what they feel is an invasion of territory such was, and still is, the case when women entered the workplace. This is particularly true for women who have sought nontraditional jobs that have previously been held by only men.

Other times, it is because a person is genuinely attracted to another person, and they cannot separate their professional behavior from their sexual instincts. And when they hear "no" from another person they feel that the other person doesn't really mean "no" to their advances, so they should, in fact, just try harder in the pursuit.

Or worse, they do not respect the feelings of the other individual and are undaunted by the rejection. The other person's feelings are irrelevant to the wishes of the perpetrator. "I always get what I want," is the motto and the motivation behind this kind of unwelcome behavior.

The behaviorial actions of the agressor becomes dangerously obsessive, particularly if the person he/she is interested in is someone they have the power to professionally manipulate. It is in this situation where a superior can completely control a subordinate. "You have to stay and work late on this project with me." "We'd better have lunch and talk about work." "You need to work this weekend."

There is also background conditioning that must be considered when attempting to understand what motivates another person to sexually harass someone at work. This is particularly true when men harass women. If a man is raised to believe that women are beneath men—second-class citizens—he may treat them as such while on the job. Or if a man's cultural and social upbringing taught him that women are sex objects, how can he possibly be doing anything wrong by pursuing a woman in his office for just that purpose?

Men that have been raised to respect people—including women—will probably never find themselves in an unpleasant situation regarding social and sexual behavior on the job. In fact, those particular men are as deeply puzzled regarding the motivation of sexual harassers as are women. Socially and sexually well-balanced people shake their heads in disgust at the behavior of those that are not.

SUPERIOR/SUBORDINATE RELATIONSHIPS

Workplace sexual harassment usually happens to women—and they have been subjected to it since they first stepped foot into the workforce. Countless women have told me their personal stories of sexual harassment, and none of them could talk about their ordeals without having their original feelings of helplessness and frustration return.

And it really didn't surprise me, when I first began researching this book, to find it was also the **mothers** of today's working women I interviewed who were compelled to pull me aside to tell me about an experience they had years ago. The stories of the mothers matched the current accounts given by their working daughters except for an important difference.

"Back then" a book like this wouldn't exist because our mothers didn't speak to anyone else about the harassment. They were often too afraid to tell anyone else what was happening to them. In fact, most married women that I spoke with, said their husbands still didn't know about the experience. Unpleasant experiences of sexual harassment on the job have been kept a secret by large numbers of women for decades. The most unsettling part of the stories I heard were the endings. Most of the women simply quit their jobs. They walked away. Many of those women wonder today what their careers would have been like if they had not been roadblocked by an act of sexual harassment. Many of the women who left their jobs naturally left them without recommendations from "the one that was chasing them around the desk."

Women being harassed thirty years ago—or even fifteen years ago—for that matter, didn't have much hope of finding a satisfactory means of ending the unwanted sexual advances they were experiencing—nor did they have much of a chance of protecting their jobs.

So although sexual harassment has always been in the workplace, it was not being acknowledged or dealt with until just a few years ago. The blame and embarrassment almost always fell on the shoulders of the woman being harassed. It is just within the past couple of years that women who have been sexually harassed are showing the courage and strength—and fortunately finding the means—to end behavior that hurts us all.

Women Harassing Men

Because more women are now in positions of authority, there are more instances of women superiors harassing male subordinates. The exact type of power threat that takes place between a male superior and woman subordinate can take place between a woman superior and a male subordinate. The men put in this position are usually at a total loss as to what they should do. Most often, the man is young and just starting out in his profession, and the woman superior is older, more established and sees herself acting as her young subordinate's "mentor." **Men who are being harassed react just like women who are being harassed.** They are shocked, insulted, confused, indignant and frightened for their jobs. And not only are these men frightened about the power the woman superior has over his job, but he is often afraid to tell anyone else because he looks like a "wimp." And being termed a wimp while you are trying to struggle up the corporate ladder is an extremely undesirable tag to have attached to the lapel of your carefully selected Brooks Brothers suit.

Harassment Has No Boundaries

Harassment can happen to anyone—by anyone. A woman or man can be harassed by a coworker, boss, client, or vendor. Men can sexually harass men just as woman can sexually harass women. And the incidents of sexual harassment can range from a subtle stare to violent rape—and even death.

The Emotional Impact of Sexual Harassment

Sexual harassment strikes down hard on a person's emotional and physical well-being. When an individual is sexually threatened or continuously exposed to the elements of a sexually hostile environment, the negative effects of such exposure or activity can physically or mentally breakdown an otherwise competent and well-adjusted individual. Depending on the degree of harassment, the emotional injuries of sexual harassment can have far-reaching and extremely damaging effects on a person.

RULE NUMBER 5: KNOW YOUR OWN COMFORT LEVEL AND RULE NUMBER 6: KNOW THE COMFORT LEVEL OF OTHERS

"Good Guys" and the Fear of Harassment

Fear of having social behavior or professional mannerisms that are truly a part of a person's work style being misconstrued by coworkers or subordinates as sexual harassment is a big concern to sensitive and "pro-people" managers. "I'm just naturally very expressive with the people who work for me," said one successful manager of a Fortune 500 firm. "I care about every member of my team, and it just seems natural to show some healthy and positive feelings to those who work for me. I'm a warm person. I'm not thinking of a person in a sexual sense when I give them a pat on the back. If I were told that I had to become a socially rigid person while at work, I really don't know if I could do my job. My working relationships with the people I work with is important to the bottom-line success of my job. I believe that by becoming a cold person—one who is overly aware of the rules of conduct regarding sexual harassment—would greatly reduce my ability to manage and motivate people."

Companies Who Care. Xerox Corporation has helped its employees define what is and isn't sexual harassment by providing employees with an initiative training program called "Shades of Grey." According to Theodore E. Payne, Manager Corporate Affirmative Action and Equal Opportunity, this program began immediately following the issuance of the 1980 EEOC guidelines. Mr. Payne states that Xerox believes in offering every means to ensure that all employees understand what those "grey areas" of sexual harassment are. "We take a firm stand on sexual harassment. We will go to whatever measures to make sure that it does not exist within our company. It is a barrier for productivity for both men and women. We don't tolerate it."

IBM, also a recognized leader in the business of understanding employee's concerns, established an equal opportunity department in 1968 to assist its employees. An extensive training program is continuously implemented regarding the issue of men and women working together on the job. IBM's "on-going commitment" policy stresses to its employees the basic rule: **Respect the individual**.

If this sound rule is kept in mind when dealing with employees, managers or coworkers will have no need to worry or fear that those they work with will ever misunderstand their intentions, behavior or work style methods.

Adding one further note to this sound philosophy of respecting the individuals you work with can be summed up simply with the word: **comfort**.

People aren't going to be concerned about experiencing sexual harassment on the job if they are being treated with personal respect and concern by those for whom they work. A good comfort level goes back to the basic need for **rule number one: Trust Your Instincts**.

Individuals on the job have an *instinctive feeling* about others around them. If you firmly establish yourself as someone who is genuinely concerned about the well-being of others, your working relationship with your subordinates and superiors will be comfortable. And such a relationship will encourage those around you to do their best.

Chapter 11

Corporate Romance: Yes, No, or Maybe?

RULE NUMBER 7: KNOW YOUR PRIORITIES

To Labor and to Love—The Case for Love on the Job

Those who insist that work is the ideal place to meet someone worthwhile—someone who shares your interests and someone you would consider dating—have a valid point. The term "job market" has taken on a different meaning during the past few years. People are really starting to sell the workplace as the ideal location to meet one's future mate, and statistics show that's exactly what is happening. People are meeting and marrying others they have met while on the job. Based on the figures regarding the number of men and women in the workplace, coupled with the number of hours both spend on the job, it's hardly a surprise that this development is taking place. According to those who promote the workplace as the ideal place to meet your future spouse, you are at your best while you're on the job. When you're at work, others get to see your skills in action; your abilities shine. Work is the place where many of your strongest assets are showcased.

The Company Social Calendar

Many companies strive to develop the team spirit of an organization by sponsoring and endorsing company functions, which include a wide range of extracurricular activities—company outings, mixers, performance and achievement clubs held in tropical resorts, softball teams, and executive board retreats for high-level management.

Companies realize that properly organized company functions that fall mainly under the heading of social gatherings are good for promoting the spirit of a company, division, or branch of an organization. It has been found that if men and women like each other and get along socially, they ultimately work better together.

Companies also are realizing that they need to make an effort to help employees strike a balance between their professional and personal lives. Stress is a major health problem facing today's working people. Companies are helping to ease this problem by encouraging people to find ways of enjoying themselves. Providing social opportunities within the framework of the company is one way employers are providing outlets for overworked employees.

As expected, however, company socializing is just one of the ways that lead to the establishment of closer, more intimate bonds between men and women who work together. Most men and women who begin dating a coworker know that it didn't require the organizing of a company event to help them initiate a relationship. Many have already taken that step. Along with the natural process of corporate courtship with coworkers comes the dilemma that often happens when men and women get together—whether it be on the job or anywhere else—breaking into couples and the forming of individual relationships.

It doesn't seem to be anyone's intention to stand in the way of true love as long as love on the job doesn't interfere with work on the job. Certain rules need to be noted when the decision is made to date or become involved with someone you meet while on the job. Meeting, dating, and even marrying someone you meet through your daily work doesn't have to be complicated, providing both individuals involved know their priorities.

A Dangerous Liasion: Superior/Subordinate Relationships

Certain relationships formed by men and women on the job immediately jeopardize jobs and long-term careers as well as endanger the environment of the workplace. When a person dates and reports to the same person, he or she is asking for trouble. The two people involved could be tremendous assets to the company, but the mere existence of their relationship automatically puts a strain on the workplace environment.

The involved superior: This person is jeopardizing his or her working relationship with other subordinates, a future with the company, and an ability to manage people objectively. This person is also putting a tremendous strain on the relationship with the involved subordinate.

The involved subordinate: In an effort to appear fair

to other employees, and to avoid being accused of showing preferential treatment, the superior might give less positive employment reviews to the involved subordinate. If, on the other hand, the involved subordinate receives positive reviews, regardless of whether his or her performance was superior before and during the affair, it is likely that others will question whether the subordinate earned high marks on the basis of ability. The involved subordinate also might be viewed by other employees as "an informant among the ranks" for the boss, and probably will experience a degree of isolation as a member of a department team.

The coworkers/the department/the company: When a superior is involved with one subordinate, others in the department are likely to feel a range of negative emotions and concerns. Resentment of the affair is a common reaction, as many workers will dislike the fact that the boss is having an affair at work, instead of supervising them. This feeling can affect a whole department or, in the extreme, an entire company. If this affair is ended, charges of sexual harassment may be brought by one of the previously involved parties, which automatically brings the company into the picture.

Considering the options: The options in a situation like this aren't that hard to figure out, although many people, when caught between their job and an affair, have a tough time facing them. Because, after all, none of them are easy. Here are a few.

Keep the relationship underground. Don't let anyone know that you are seeing each other, but plan on spending a lot of time and energy concealing something that others may eventually find out, anyway.

Someone leaves the company. Is the relationship important enough to both of you to consider making changes in either or both of your careers? This is where priorities need to be very clear.

Do nothing until management mentions it. It is better for the two people to decide who is going to leave the department or company rather than let things get to the point where the company has to make the decision for you. More positive results can be achieved if the couple approaches management before management approaches them. Companies like to help responsible couples find a good solution—and the solution could enable both employees to stay with the company.

RULE NUMBER 8: ESTABLISH CLEAR BOUNDARIES

Dating Coworkers

Some people simply won't get involved with anyone at work. Others are a little more relaxed on that policy but are very careful about who they get involved with on the job. Then there are others who view their jobs as a shopping mall of opportunities for either brief affairs, long-term involvements or possible mates. Each position involves making personal decisions based upon your priorities. Dating someone at work is okay as long as the relationship takes the following guidelines into consideration.

1. Don't abuse the privileges of the workplace by misusing time and expense money to pursue a personal relationship.

2. Try to keep your relationship with a coworker private. You are only hurting yourself by discussing it

with other coworkers. The person you are dating should behave in the same manner and respect your need for confidentiality.

3. Follow the proper ways of approaching someone that you are interested in seeing socially. Be very clear and upfront about your desire to see someone on a social rather than professional level.

Chapter 12

Personal Styles of Communication

"It's hard to believe seven years ago I was terrified to tell anyone," said Miss Neville "That was one of the mistakes I made in my workplace. And, I didn't tell anyone because I worked with all men. I guess it was an acknowledgment that something bad was happening to me. I didn't want to be office gossip."

Buffalo News
June 26, 1988

RULE NUMBER 9: LEARN HOW TO LET OTHERS KNOW HOW YOU FEEL

Talking to Andrea Brookman, another employee of Taft Broadcasting, while we were in Toronto, was the right thing for me to do. It's unfortunate that she didn't work for the same television station I did. Had there been other women within my department at Channel 2, especially women like Andrea, I am sure I would have been able to talk to them, and I would have been able to count on them for some support. Unfortunately for me, in those days there were none.

I now advise people who are being seriously harassed on the job to let someone else at work know about it. I really believe that one of my male colleagues just might have been concerned about my situation. I thought I was being a professional by not letting anyone around me know what was happening. Instead, I chose a nonconfrontational position by suffering in silence and counting on one person—Jim Conshafter—to "save me." The reasoning behind my decision was that I didn't want to create gossip; I didn't want to cause a stir within my department. And, of course, in addition to my professional reasons, I didn't want to face the personal embarrassment I thought making it known would cause me. I was ashamed and embarrassed that it was happening to me—and, worse, that I didn't really know how to handle it. I failed on three important communication efforts.

Obviously the first had to do with Cochran. I simply and clearly did not get the message across to him that what he was doing to me was wrong and that I did not like it—and, in fact, that for his own sake as well as mine, he needed to stop. Even though I thought I was being very clear—in fact at the time, I didn't think I could be any clearer—I was not successful in making him realize that what he was doing was wrong and that his advances were unwelcome. Therefore, I can only conclude that my communication efforts failed.

Many victims of sexual harassment have tearfully related to me how they insisted over and over again that they be left alone, and how they told pursuers to "cut it out." But, sadly enough, in such emotional situations, individuals tend to focus on what is going on within themselves internally and not what they are actually saying to the other person. On closer examination of verbal messages sent by people to someone who was harassing them, I found that, although there existed behind their words overwhelming feelings of fear and outrage, the actual message delivered to the culprit lacked the strength required to prompt the harasser to stop. Without question, the basic goal of someone being harassed is for the act to stop taking place. Communication is the only way to reach that goal successfully.

My second communication sin was committed when I made my formal report to Jim Conshafter. I didn't stress to Conshafter that my report to him required his immediate attention and resolution. I assumed that because he was a high-level manager, he would act on my report. Not only should you never assume that a superior knows how to respond correctly to each situation, you also should know that he or she will only take as much action as he or she feels your situation requires. You are the only person who can communicate to management properly and adequately the nature and severity of your own problem.

My final communication error was in failing to let my colleagues know about the problem I was facing and further, to let them know how upset I was about the wrongful actions that were taking place. You don't necessarily need to involve coworkers in your own dilemma, but you do need to make the people around you aware that something illegal is going on. Not only can they offer needed support, they also can offer important contemporaneous facts to management later should there be an internal investigation. In her cartoon strip "Cathy," contemporary cartoonist Cathy Guisewite has Cathy facing sexual harassment by her boss and shows how she solved it before it became a real problem. Cathy knew enough to tell the receptionist what had happened to her. She calculated correctly that the receptionist would "communicate" her boss's inappropriate behavior to the entire Western hemisphere.

Most important, by letting some coworkers know that you are experiencing unwelcome harassment, you are making the statement that you do not condone this type of behavior. Later, no one can say that the harassment behavior must not have bothered you or that, God forbid, you actually encouraged it.

Failing to communicate

The biggest communication problem faced by today's companies has nothing to do with letting the public know who they are. By watching television, we all know that "GE brings good things to life," just as we are also aware of the onslaught of other image messages sent us, each day, by the thousands of other companies using the airwaves and print media to communicate to us. No, communicating corporate messages these days is not a problem. Properly directing millions of advertising and marketing dollars can take care of that easily.

And, although major chunks of public relations budgets are being spent annually by corporations to communicate and encourage open lines of communication between employees and employers, these corporate efforts still do not solve the most serious corporate communications problem. Reaching employees through seminars, training sessions, newsletters, attitude studies, department surveys, annual reports, and newsletters does not solve the wide variety of individual communication problems that eventually and regularly cause major problems for both the corporation and its employees.

It is not surprising that the real—and crippling—communication breakdown in companies is *among* employees. Working people have trouble communicating with each other, whether it be with another coworker or a boss. The most prevalent complaint individuals have about their jobs usually pertains to a communication problem. Most people will be extremely vocal with people outside the workplace—friends and family—regarding their problems on the job, but that is where their communication stops. Those bringing home tales of woe about our jobs usually hear, but don't listen, to the advice we are given: GO TELL THE PERSON HOW YOU FEEL. LET THE PERSON KNOW WHAT'S BOTHERING YOU.

We usually don't tell a coworker/superior what's on our minds, because we don't know how to say it or where to say it or even when to say it. We are afraid that we may say it incorrectly, so we decide to do nothing, to ride it out. Rather than speaking up, we keep it inside. And so we let it eat at us—and by doing this, we only hurt ourselves.

Behind the communication problem

One reason most of us have trouble communicating our feelings to others on the job is because we are conditioned to believe that the workplace is best kept a nonemotional environment. Before women entered the workplace, the men in gray suits who built corporate America certainly weren't sitting around the conference table, or anywhere else for that matter, talking about their sensitivity and revealing their deepest emotions to one another. When women arrived on the job, they were told to keep their feelings to themselves; in fact, they were even encouraged to camouflage. So they donned tie blouses and dark suits and vowed that no tears would be shed in any corner of the office.

We women all believed that in order to be true professionals, we could not and should not show our feelings in the workplace. To get emotional or cry on the job was career suicide. Even though we now recognize that we are sensitive creatures between the hours of nine and five, we still can't get over the original fear of showing our emotions. So, when something happens on the job that has to do with our feelings or goes against our moral standards, we don't know how to react. We don't know how to express these feelings.

We don't like to think that our professional life is emotion-packed. We like to think that feelings belong within our personal lives only. But the basic flaw in that theory is that we all care deeply about our jobs, they mean a lot to us. They are the yardstick we—and others—use to determine whether we are a success. Our jobs make the difference in whether we live in a nice house. Jobs buy us status symbols, give us power, and lead us to better standards of living. Our jobs define us. We care desperately about them.

When it comes to having to talk to management about such issues as social relationships or sexual harassment or any type of social-sexual activity, most of us are completely lost. There have never have been any rules telling men or women how to discuss such behavior in a professional and sensitive manner. Even though a person may finally be able to identify and acknowledge the interference of feelings on the job, it is still difficult to figure out how to communicate those feelings to someone else, particularly without being misunderstood. Effective interpersonal communication on the job is an art, and few people know how to do it properly.

During the workday, all of us could get along much better—and certainly work together more productively—if we understood the unspoken intentions of others. In addition to letting others know what we are feeling, we should let others tell us what they are feeling as well.

The art of interpersonal communication

There is a big difference in the way we express ourselves to our superiors and the way we address others at our own level in the company. Good communication is extremely important, particularly when our reasons for initiating a discussion have to do with such critical topics as salaries, job performance, or any other problems we are experiencing on the job. When communicating to other employees at work, as simple as it may sound, remember who you are talking to—know your audience and how to reach it. Realize you will be held responsible for what you say. People remember what you say and respond either negatively or positively to your statements. Yes, you are judged by your coworkers and managers by what you say. Know and remember who you are talking to—your job is on the line.

Great speakers know their audience. They know their language and they know how to relay their intended message. Even controversial topics can be addressed successfully when they are presented by an adept speaker who is skilled in the four important elements of effective speaking: **direction, demeanor, delivery and details.**

Direction. What point are you trying to make? Don't go off on a tangent. If you are talking to your superior about something as important as sexual harassment, don't clutter the conversation with other "oh-by-the-ways" that have been bugging you and have nothing to do with the problem of sexual harassment. Be direct. Stay targeted.

Demeanor. If you appear casual in your body language or happen to be perched on an armchair and swinging your leg while you are talking about a serious social/sexual problem, your body language is telling quite another story. Although you are probably nervous, this is not the time to shrug shoulders, adjust clothing, or laugh.

Delivery. Speak clearly. Be very precise in what you are saying. Make your point but don't appear threatening. Employ good professional conduct. Regardless of how upset you are about what has happened, it is very important that you appear to be in control. Let the person you are talking to know that you have given this problem a lot of thought.

Don't use vague terms and don't assume the person you are addressing has any idea what you are talking about. Not only are you relaying an experience to another person, you also are asking for specific action. The person you are addressing needs to hear you ask for that action.

Details. It is often painful for the person speaking to go into details regarding sexual harassment or any other kind of social/sexual problem on the job, but it is a must. Not only does it go on record that you reported everything that was troubling you, but it allows the person receiving the report to know all the facts that will help him or her take the necessary and immediate action you are asking for. Failure to give details may suggest the absence of them, which could intimate to the person to whom you are reporting the grievance that you have no cause for complaining. Your report will be evaluated based on details. Be ready to provide them.

Whenever you are making any official report to management, you must

Be clear
Be definite
Be reasonable and rational
Be confident

Know your audience

There are four basic groups of audiences (or people we communicate with) at work:

- **management** those above us
- **peers** those around us, those who share the same rank and often compete with us for promotions and positions
- **subordinates** those people who report to us
- **outsiders** those outside of our immediate company, people whom we deal with professionally, such as customers, vendors and the general public

The more power a person has over your livelihood, the more careful you should be about what you say to that person. Knowing your audience is based on common sense—use it when you are dealing with people who can literally change your life.

RULE NUMBER 10: KNOW WHEN—AND HOW—TO SPEAK UP

There is a time, a place, and a way in which to report any kind of social/sexual behavior, especially sexual harassment, that is interfering with your work or the overall well-being of your department. The term whistleblower is given to those employees who report another employee(s) for wrongdoing. Whether to report sexual misconduct or the existence of a social/sexual relationship that is interfering with the workplace is a difficult decision. If you conduct yourself in a professional manner and understand how the process works, your task will be easier. If you communicate clearly, you can reduce and even eliminate any hint that you might be saying something for personal gain.

Before reporting:

1. Do a quiet check beforehand and make sure you are going to the right place to report it. Most companies have established grievance procedures—find out how yours works. If you are in a small company without set procedures, go directly to the top person; he/she is the person who cares the most about the business.
2. Reflect on the reason you feel you need to report someone else's behavior. Is there real validity to what you are saying? Do you have solid details to support your concern? Do you have any hidden reasons for reporting this person (or persons) other than your named concern? Be honest with yourself. Reporting someone else is a serious action, and you must be confident in your need to take such a step.

In the case of sexual harassment, most employees who experience it are very clear on what they are feeling; they just have a great deal of trouble figuring out a way to communicate those feelings to someone else. My biggest problem with my experience was that I had difficulty talking about it. Being a private person, I am reluctant to talk about my personal feelings. Know ahead of time how you are going to share your story.

Timing

Make an appointment, even if it is only for later in the same day. Make it official business. Don't drop in on the person. Chances are the person already has a set agenda, hundreds of other things on his or her mind, and could be extremely distracted with other projects or concerns. Your complaint may subconsciously serve as a nuisance in an already too busy day.

Making an appointment will allow the other person to give your concern the proper attention. You will also alert that person that you have something important to discuss. If you just show up unexpectedly, your action could be viewed as impulsive, and may not be taken as seriously.

Also to your advantage—by having a time set aside —you know that you will be able to have an uninterrupted talk, making a difficult task less daunting.

While on the importance of timing—once you feel you are being bothered by a particular type of social/sexual behavior in the office, report it immediately. Don't wait. Legal cases of sexual harassment have been lost because a person waited too long to make a report.

The place

Arrange for the meeting to take place in a quiet office or area in which you feel comfortable. Be sure the setting is professional. Don't talk to someone in management about such a sensitive issue at a bar, while having lunch, in the hall, while seated next to the person at a company function, or, worst of all, don't interrupt a project to launch into your dilemma.

The reporting should take place when the management representative is prepared to talk only about your problem. Mentioning it in any other less suitable setting will diminish your own concerns and will look like an afterthought on your part rather than the official reporting it should and needs to be.

How to say it

Before you go into the meeting, sort out your feelings and be very clear about what you are going to say. This is no time to be vague or to use expressions such as "he sort of put his hand on my knee." Did he or didn't he put his hand on your knee? Use words that say what you mean—and say them in a way that reveals that you mean them. For instance . . .

The opening: "I appreciate your taking the time to talk to me about a problem I am experiencing here at work. I am coming to you because Jack's behavior toward me is interfering with my ability to perform my job."

The facts: "Last week, while I was working late on the Dynamics proposal [or whatever work activity you were engaged in when it happened] Jack said... or did. . .to me." "Then, he said. . .and I responded by telling him to leave me alone."

Your feelings: "Mr. Green, I was shocked and deeply offended by Jack's actions. This type of behavior is offensive to me and makes it very difficult for me to do my job."

Team player reinforcement: "As you know, I take my job and my position with this company very seriously. I normally enjoy my work and have found this to be a great place to work. I came to you today because I knew that I could talk to you—and I knew you would understand. I wanted to do the right thing."

Asking for help: "I am asking you to help me solve this problem. I don't believe I can handle it by myself. I need your help in correcting Jack's behavior and preventing it from happening again."

As part of your appeal for help, include the following:

- Set up a follow-up meeting.
- Document your conversation.
- Confirm with the person you reported it to that he or she was the right person to discuss your grievance with.
- Be definite about the kind of help you are seeking.
- Let your employer know you are amenable to working things out. It is not the company you are upset with—it is the individual(s).
- Carefully let your employer know that you found the behavior so serious that you felt the need to document it and have kept a journal of times, dates, and the nature of the incidents.
- Without any hint of a threat, let the person to whom you are reporting know that you expect the behavior to be corrected.
- To prevent the manager you reported the incidents to from joining forces with the manager you are reporting, it is a good idea to send a written and confidential follow-up letter to him or her that basically reiterates the problem and your concerns. This legitimizes your report and protects you from man-

agement collusion. Keep the tone of your letter positive. Thank the person for his or her time and concern.

If you are a manager receiving a report:

- Take all reporting seriously, because it is.
- Ignoring someone's report won't make that person go away. Respond immediately.
- If you don't know about your company's policy regarding such matters, find out what it is quickly.
- Document the complete report.
- Report the complaint to someone above you. Let your supervisors know what is going on; if you don't implement proper action, they are the ones who will ultimately be responsible for your treatment of the situation.
- If you are with a large company, speak to someone in authority within the human resources division. Get guidance.

SEEKING SOLUTIONS THROUGH COMMUNICATION

Most people who report sexual harasment aren't interested in causing trouble, they are interested in ending it. If management seeks out corrective resolution immediately, the chances of keeping the human resource damages to a minimum are enhanced. If harassment is reported promptly and corrected in a timely fashion, it can be looked upon by all parties merely as a misunderstanding.

If, however, the company finds that sexual harassment

of a serious nature took place, it is likely that the company will terminate the offender. It is important that the company communicate clearly with the offender as well as the workplace victim. The person being fired must understanding clearly what company policy he or she violated and the severity of the act(s) committed. The person who made the report should be kept apprised of what is being done by the proper managers. The victim is still going to be upset about what took place, and although the perpetrator may have been released, the victim is going to be fearful that the company will no longer look favorably upon him or her for making such a report, and may worry about retaliation. Smart managers will let the offended parties know that they are valuable employees, not troublemakers.

ANOTHER WAY TO SPEAK UP

If you find that someone else's behavior is affecting not just you but others in the office as well, it is wise to report your concern as a group. This is an extremely safe and low-risk way to report behavior such as a disruptive office affair between a superior and a coworker, or the behavior of a group of people rather than just one individual, such as in the case of creating a hostile and sexist workplace environment. The report will be taken quite seriously and will be viewed as a professional decision made by a group of concerned workers. Have more than one spokesperson. Don't allow the attention to be focused on one person within your group.

TO SPEAK OR NOT TO SPEAK

Many people have said that if sexual harassment is happening to you on the job, you should just leave. "Get another job," they say. That's easier said than done if you live in a small town that perhaps has only a few industries. It's also rather difficult to switch jobs when you are in a specialized field. Few people being sexually harassed happen to live in a major metropolitan area, possess terrific credentials, and don't care whether they lose their seniority with a company they have been with for years.

Only you, the individual can assess your situation. Sometimes leaving a company is an alternative, providing you have other valid reasons for leaving a job, such as you have found a better job. But in many cases, people don't have other jobs to go to. They need the job they have, even when it means facing sexual harassment.

Reporting someone else's behavior on the job has to be a personal decision. People have to make their own evalutions regarding how much another person's behavior is adversely affecting them. We all have different levels of tolerance, and only we can determine when something is bothering us enough to force us into taking some sort of action.

MAKE THE EFFORT

In order to be successful at our jobs, each of us needs to strive continually toward better communication on the job. Good communication doesn't create problems—it prevents them. Communication is not just a tool for expressing dissatisfaction. It also boosts job satisfaction when we hear from others that all-important ring of positive feedback. The most successful managers know how important it is to care enough about the people who work for them to spend the few minutes a day it takes to let others know how they feel about the work they are doing. When they are happy with an individual's performance, they let that person know. That is not sophisticated corporate communications at all, but merely an example of a good manager exercising good interpersonal communication skills.

Chapter 13:

More about Men and Sexual Harassment

Although men and women in a recent survey of business-school students generally agree on what constituted sexual harassment, they sharply disagreed over how they thought women would react to it. Of the men, 46% said they thought women would be flattered by sexual harassment; 5% of the women agreed.

Delaney Kirk Survey
Wall Street Journal
August 8, 1988

Most men are uneasy about sexual harassment.

Some men are concerned that they might be doing something to offend the women they work with, while others are angry that they even need to worry about it all. It's a nuisance some men say, that they even have to be bothered with talk of rules about social and sexual behavior. A woman who spends a good deal of her time lecturing to corporations about sexual harassment usually hears a few men grumble as they enter into the conference room for their mini-course on harassment. Often during the conference, the female lecturer will even hear comments that easily could be construed as sexual harassment.

Whether or not a man's behavior ever falls under the category of sexual harassment is becoming a growing concern to intelligent men in positions of management—particularly to those who are relatively new at the business of managing women.

And, although women are usually the victims of sexual harassment, it is men who have the most questions about the behavior. Here are the most common questions men have about sexual harassment.

Why do woman fear sexual harassment?

Women fear sexual harassment because it is a form of behavior that imposes a threat. Just like any sexual assault, whether it's physical or verbal, it makes them feel powerless and vulnerable. It is a violation in the truest sense because it asks a woman to surrender sexually for the sake of someone's else's demands. Once a woman realizes that she is falling victim to sexual harassment, her instinct is to run away. Unfortunately, when jobs and livelihoods are at stake, running away is not always an option. Not only does a woman fear sexual harassment because it is a sexual violation, but she is alarmed because it can create havoc with her career.

Sexual harassment has nothing to do with how a woman feels about men in general. Many men believe that a woman who is upset about sexual harassment doesn't like men, or has hang-ups about them. After my experience with sexual harassment, many men made the comment to me that I really must hate men. I liked men before the sexual harassment started, while it was going on, and after the harassment was over. The only thing I didn't like was my boss's sexual advances toward me while I was at work.

Isn't sexual harassment really just one more discrimination complaint women have against men?

No. Although the claim of sexual harassment under the law falls under Title VII, which prohibits discrimination because of sex, it really is like no other form of illegal job behavior because it also can be viewed as a sexual crime depending upon its intensity.

Sexual harassment is looked upon as discrimination because the person who is being sexually harassed is usually being harassed because of her sex. Further discrimination takes place when the harassment victim is denied promotions, loses her job or is treated differently because of her reaction to the harassment.

How can I let a woman know I would never do anything improper?

It is relatively easy to let someone know she can trust you: Behave properly.

If you ever feel that a woman is uneasy about your behavior, you can reassure her that you would never consider behaving improperly toward her.

Men who are good at managing people usually don't ever need to tell a woman openly that she can count on him to behave properly. Because of his keen sensitivity and respect for her as an employee, she already knows she can trust him.

Look at the way women dress—aren't they asking for someone to take a shot at them?

Although not all women dress appropriately for work, what a women wears to work is not an invitation for sexual advances. In some cases, victims of sexual harassment did dress provocatively and unfortunately gave the appearance of welcoming sexual come-ons.

But regardless of the woman's attire in the workplace, fashion and dress do not signal that it is okay to harass a woman sexually. Never is it appropriate to harass a person because of the way he or she dresses. In most companies, that would hardly be a valid argument when charges of harassment are raised.

How will I know if I am guilty of harassing a woman coworker?

There are three simple ways to know if you are guilty of harassment.

First—you *alone* will know what your real intentions are. Men know when they might be harassing a woman because they instinctively know when the advances are unwelcome—and sexual harassment is all about the term "unwelcome." Pursuing a woman who works for or with you is not the same as pursuing a woman outside the work environment. Within the workplace, the pursuit cannot exist, otherwise it could be cited as sexual harassment particularly if the woman is not interested in a personal relationship with the pursuer.

The second indicator of a woman feeling harassed is changes in her behavior. If she seems uncomfortable in your presence, changes her work patterns, seems withdrawn and unfriendly, and actually avoids being alone with you—she is probably feeling harassed.

Third, the simple and surest way to know whether you are guilty of harassment is to become familiar with the rules regarding proper social and sexual behavior on the job and to see whether you are breaking any of them.

After dating a coworker, could I ever be accused of harassing her?

Yes. Regardless of any previous relationship in which two people have willingly engaged in the past, if there are unwelcome advances *now*, then someone in the relationship could be guilty of sexual harassment.

If she wants nothing to do with you after a relationship is over, and you continue to pursue her, you may find yourself being accused of sexual harassment.

The way to protect yourself, and your job, once a relationship with a coworker is *over is to make it clear to her that you understand the relationship is over and that you will only view her as a coworker from that point on.* Without emotion, and as difficult as it may be, you must follow the strictest of rules when it comes to dealing professionally with the woman you shared a close relationship with at one time. Remember: Your job is at stake.

If I don't touch a woman, how can I be guilty of harassment?

You don't need to touch a woman to be guilty of sexual harassment. Sexual harassment also includes improper comments and prolonged staring. (See chapter 10, Definitions that Draw Lines.)

If I pursue a woman, on my own time and outside the office, how can that be considered harassment?

Sexual harassment of a coworker often takes place outside the office. If a woman works for the same company you do, you can be charged with harassment regardless of where the harassment takes place.

In fact, there are cases of sexual harassment where an outside client, vendor, or supplier can be guilty of sexually harassing someone. Although these situations are more complicated, they are legitimate instances of sexual harassment because they are part of the daily activity of doing business, and they have the same impact and consequences as primary sexual harassment. These acts have to do with *power* over another person and they are *unwanted* and *unwelcome.*

How do I respond when I've been charged with sexual harassment?

If a formal complaint has not been filed:

If you are fortunate enough to have a woman approach you first to discuss her feelings regarding your behavior toward her, you have a good chance of correcting a very delicate situation before it gets to the damaging stages. Obviously, if a woman brings up her discomfort regarding your behavior, then she feels she is being harassed. At this point, it is important to find out exactly what is troubling her. Get the specifics. If it truly is a misunderstanding, then let her know you had no idea you were making her uncomfortable. Apologize for any discomfort and be very careful in the future about how you deal with this person—on every level. Also, document your conversation with the woman, because, in the event that your discussion did not ease her mind, she may proceed further with her complaint by going to your manager. It is important at this point, that you show you had no intention of (1) making unwelcome advances or (2) discriminating or treating this individual in a different manner from the way you would any other employee.

If a formal complaint has been filed:

If you find yourself in the precarious situation of already having had a sexual harassment claim filed against you within your company, you will have to be ready to answer very specific questions about your behavior toward the woman who raised the complaint. You will certainly be asked about the actual charges of harassment and your overall treatment of her as an employee probably will be scrutinized. Any performance evaluations you made during the alleged period of harassment could be compared to those made out before the period in question.

Because you are the only person who really knows what your intentions are regarding the employee who raised the charges, it is up to you to do your own personal assessment of the situation, and then proceed accordingly.

If the charges are not serious, it is in everyone's best interest that, under the company's supervision, you apologize to the woman and assure her that nothing of that nature will ever occur again. This puts the situation behind both of you. In addition, no one else in the workplace need ever know there was a problem, providing the woman did not feel it was blatant harassment and had not told other coworkers about it

If her charges are valid, you probably will find yourself at the mercy of the company's policy and procedures regarding those found guilty of illegal behavior on the job.

If I have ever find myself doing something that could be considered sexual harassment of a coworker, how can I correct my errors of the past with that particular woman—or can I?

The best policy to follow—if you feel you may have said or done something inappropriate to a woman at work—is to call yourself on it *immediately*. By simply saying you are sorry and you realize you may have said or done something that she may have felt was unacceptable, you protect yourself from having your actions or words misunderstood.

Situations that could have become sexual harassment are checked everyday by men who realize that they may have said or done the wrong thing. Letting a mistake go—because you don't think it was important enough—could indicate to a woman that you have a pattern of doing or saying such things and you will continue to offend her. Although it may seem unnecessary to simply make an apology for your behavior—it's worth it if it will save your place in the company later.

How can I safely ask someone out from my office?

There are certain situations you should stay completely away from when it comes to dating someone from your company. The first situation is the superior/subordinate relationship. You should not date your boss nor should you date someone who reports to you. Although people do, it is an explosive situation, and usually causes problems both for the couple and for other employees within the workplace environment.

The classic case of a superior/subordinate relationship is the executive and his or her secretary. Although this involvement has been going on for decades, it still spells trouble—especially in large corporations where it is particularly frowned upon by top management.

There is no safe advice for those who venture into these relationships. They may work sometimes but the risks are very high. In fact, in my opinion, they're too high.

Dating a coworker, particularly someone who is in an another department, is different from dating a superior. Although there are still some career risks when a person makes the decision to date someone from the same company, it is possible to date, become involved and perhaps even marry someone you may meet on the job. **The key to**

these situations is not only your approach, but also your ability to manage the relationship.

There is only one safe way to ask a woman out who works for the same company you do. Even though you must risk your pride in the event that there is no interest, it is best to be very up front and extremely direct in showing your interest in pursuing a dating relationship. Don't attempt to feel a woman out by suggesting that you get together to talk about a project—don't try to fake a "work" excuse to see someone when you have other intentions. You need to come right out and say you would like to see her socially—*outside of work*—and you wonder if she would be comfortable in doing so. This approach may cut short the first few steps of the "mating dance" but in the longer term, it is safer and more responsible behavior between two people who work together.

If she says she doesn't date people from work, respect her policy. In fact, if she says no for any reason, let it go. Although your male instincts may tell you to keep pursuing, this isn't the time or place to act upon them. You also must be careful that you don't treat her differently after she has turned you down. Some people might sabotage another's work when they have been rejected or slighted. Any form of retaliation can be viewed as sexual harassment at a later date.

If she agrees to see you socially, and you both find yourself headed toward a serious relationship, there will soon come a time when you both need to talk about how to keep your personal relationship under control while at work. You will also need to talk about priorities. (See chapter 10, Definitions that Draw Lines.)

Our office is small and very informal. Aren't the rules on sexual harassment more lenient for small companies?

Sexual harassment is sexual harassment no matter where it takes place. The major difference between small companies and large corporations is the dynamics of the team. The fewer the people in a company, the greater the opportunity there is to establish closer friendships and to establish better, more direct means of communication.

How can I tell another guy at work to stop harassing the women in the office without sounding like a moral policeman?

The best way to tell a coworker to stop harassing women is simply to tell him to knock it off. If his harassment is obvious to you, it is certainly blatant harassment and needs to cease immediately.

PART THREE:

INSIDE THE SYSTEM

Chapter 14

Hold Your Applause

"I'm glad I've seen that done," thought Alice. "I've so often read in the newspapers, at the end of trials, 'There was some attempt at applause, which was immediately suppressed by the officers of the court,' and I never understood what it meant till now."

Alice's Adventures in Wonderland
Lewis Carroll

Courtrooms no longer impress me. But if they still did, I would have been impressed with the Court of Appeals building at Foley Square in New York City, where my hearing was being held.

Oral arguments had been set for May 22, 1987, and the team of lawyers representing me was well prepared. The brief that had been submitted previously by my lawyers, Jim Meyerson and Jonathan Moore, had been brilliant.

Meyerson and Moore were experts in the field of Title VII law, and it was evident by the way they had approached every aspect of my case. The problem, the Manhattan team of lawyers had told me up front, was that they hadn't agreed with the way my case was presented to the district court in Buffalo. In an appeal, no new evidence can be presented, so they felt they had much to overcome when presenting the case to the three judges presiding on the bench of the court of appeals.

Thea and I watched as Frank Stewart entered the courtroom. He had not lost his charm; he was as smooth as ever when he delivered his oral argument. The only thing that disturbed the flow of his performance was a sudden interruption. The oldest judge present pulled off his glasses, stretched his neck out, and peered down over the bench.

"Now, Mr. Stewart, now, I've just noticed something here," interrupted the judge. "Could you or can you possibly tell me, can anyone tell me—why a decision wasn't reached on this case for over two years?"

Stewart folded his hands behind his back and dramtically puffed out his chest. He was probably wondering why the judge was asking him. He seemed annoyed that he had been interrupted, especially when he probably thought his prepared statements were moving along so well.

Stewart looked around the courtroom as though someone else might step in and answer the judge's intrusive question. "I'm sorry, your honor, but I really have no idea," Stewart responded back to the judge rather dryly and formally.

"Oh, I see," said the judge lightly, as though Stewart's answer had satisfied him. The judge put his glasses back on and settled in to hear the rest of Frank Stewart's argument. The Taft attorney's statement seemed brief, and when he finished, he closed his notebook firmly as though he was annoyed that he had had to deal with this case once more.

Jim Meyerson quietly walked to the front of the courtroom and began to speak.

I was overwhelmed by the sensitive and sincere words my attorney was now delivering. In the almost seven years that I had been unwillingly exposed to Title VII law, I had never heard nor read such a solid and moving argument given for the sake of fairness. Jim Meyerson's words forced any listener to consider why all of us must be concerned with the issue of an individual's rights. In just a few minutes, Jim had uncovered the real issue that had become buried deep within all the mounds and piles of documents that now made up case *CIV-82-622C, Neville versus Taft Broadcasting Company.*

Without dramatic gestures or posturing, he spoke strongly about things I knew he truly believed in. I realized it wasn't just Thea and me who were captivated by his words. It became obvious that he had grabbed the attention and respect of all three of the high court judges. Jim made a very clear distinction between harassment cases and other kinds of discrimination cases. He set forth the illogical result of Judge Curtin's decision. How on earth, he said, could Judge Curtin have found that I was physically harassed and that sexual favors to my supervisor were a prerequisite to continued employment at Taft—and at the same time find that my employer was not in any way responsible or liable for any resulting damage to me?

By this time I knew enough about courtrooms to know when judges were interested in what they were hearing, and when they were not. I was certain Jim had the undivided attention of the judges before him.

When both attorneys were finished presenting their case, one of the judges cleared his throat—uncomfortably it seemed to me—and began to speak. I knew from the sound of his apologetic tone, that the decision wasn't going to be what I wanted.

"We realize that the plaintiff was harassed, and we are sorry." For a moment, my heart lurched. It was the first time anyone had told me he was sorry. "Unfortunately," the judge continued carefully, "the court of appeals is not designed to correct the errors made at trial level—particularly, and especially, those made by trial attorneys."

While the other two justices nodded in agreement, the judge went on to say that the arguments presented that morning were extraordinary. But I wasn't sure if Jim Meyerson caught the judge's final complimentary remark. Abruptly, he turned away from the bench and left the courtroom.

Thea and I found him on a bench in the city park next to the mammoth court building. It was apparent he was too upset to talk. I wanted to console him but knew that I couldn't because I was feeling the same way he was. I remembered the first time I had met him. He had agreed to meet me at his office in New York on a Sunday. While we were discussing my appeal in his modest conference room, he unconsciously toyed with a tarnished but sturdy set of "lady justice" scales that sat upon his meeting table. Prodded by the light touch of his fingers, the old scales had moved up and down while we talked. It was obvious that he was a lawyer who was motivated by justice rather than his own financial gain.

I was sure there weren't many of his kind around. He specialized in an area of law that often subjected him to the pain and heartache he was feeling today. As unpleasant as it had been for me, I hoped this was my last experience with the court system. But to Jim Meyerson, this area of law was his whole life.

While Thea, Jim and I sat together quietly talking about what had happened in court, a woman attorney whom Jim knew stopped by to talk. Thea whispered to me that she was a well-known civil rights attorney. According to Thea, she had worked hard to defend the rights of prisoners in Attica.

Still upset, Jim told the woman a little bit about my case. She shook her head and turned to look at me. "It's a tough system—it's hard to believe in it," she said roughly. "In fact, I recommend that you don't. In my job, I'm constantly beating my head against the wall. Try to forget what's happened to you—the best thing to do is just to go on with your life."

I didn't answer her, but nodded as though I was considering what she had said. I knew she was right. Getting on with my life was all I wanted to do. She said good-bye and left. She obviously was working on a case, and in a hurry, I thought. In spite of what she had told me, I suspected she was a fighter and probably would never stop believing in her work.

The judges returned with a decision on the same day as the oral arguments. Jim Meyerson sent a copy of the decision to me the next week.

May 22, 1987

Dear Kathleen,

No sooner did I get back to my office on this date after you and Thea had calmed me down, did I receive a telephone call from the Clerk of the Second Circuit; and I was informed that the case had been affirmed. I said that I was flabbergasted because I had just argued the same; and he indicated that it was unusual to receive a decision immediately. It is probably not unusal. However, for whatever cowardly reason, the Circuit elected not to summarily affirm while we were present; instead they stroked us—me specifically, although, as you know, the one judge said that the arguments were good although I took such with a grain of salt. I do not believe Stewart's presentation was good at all, although, in terms of results, it was obviously effective.

What can I say? You know that, before you calmed me down, I predicted a loss; said your odds had changed from 100 to 1 to 1000 to 1. The judge's last comments just played their hand. I flushed them out, by and large, it was apparent that they did not want to deal with the case. The comment about the delay in the trial decision was interesting, but obviously cosmetic. The circuit really elected not to address the issues. The process has become dishonest. The atmosphere brought on by Reagan has permeated the bench; and I must say, I am very disheartened.

The burden which you must feel is, in itself, tremendous; and I am only sorry that the result was not better; the process not more fair. Really, very, very sad.

As the attorney, Liz (whom you met in the park), indicated, you must put it behind you and go forward. I suppose, at some level—perhaps even significant, your life has been altered in a way unlikely ever to be undone; and one would hope that, in a system of justice which claims to be so great, something more honest, at least in the process, would come out of the same. Even though we lost, I would have felt much better if the issues raised were addressed head on, and that we were told our logic/analysis/evaluation were wrong. Now we are made to feel as if we have no substance whatsoever; and such is hurting to me and I know to you.

It is apparent that judges are refusing, if at all possible, not to move the law in any direction, which, in effect, is taking the law backwards.

So be it. If at all possible, try and keep the faith. Your struggle and courage are not for naught. I wish you could have received something from it. Do not lose faith.

Sincerely,

James Meyerson

Attached to Jim's letter, was a copy of the decision. Instead of the 40 page decision Curtin had handed down, this decision was only one page:

> "Although Neville established a prima facie case of quid pro quo sexual harassment under Title VII, we agree with Chief Judge Curtin that Taft rebutted her claim by demonstrating legitimate business reasons for her termination.
>
> . . .As to Neville's assertion [regarding] Cochran's sexual advances ...Chief Judge Curtin characterized Cochran's activities as merely "disquieting."

I folded up the single page of the decision. Once, again, as far as I was concerned the wrong standard of law had been affirmed but my days of fighting back were now over.

STARTING OVER

July 1987

One night in July, while going through my mail, I found a nice note from Jim Meyerson expressing his sympathy that I was being forced to appear in court, again. I didn't know what he was talking about—my case was over.

Attached to his note was a photocopy of a notice from Judge Curtin stating that I was to appear in his court the next day. The offical court document said I was being asked to pay for Taft Broadcasting's court costs. As Taft was the prevailing party in a lawsuit, apparently there was some sort of federal rule that would allow the company to exercise that privilege. Obviously, they had.

I noticed that the subpeona had been served upon Joe several weeks earlier, yet I had heard nothing from his office. Thea no longer worked there, so I needed to call Joe to find out what was going on in Judge Curtin's court in Buffalo.

Early the next day, I called Joe from Washington and asked him if there was something he forgot to tell me. He said he was on his way out the door, and had not realized that today was the day I was due in court. He told me to call the court—myself—and see if I could obtain a postponement. I called the court clerk and soon realized that he was not going to budge. He expected me to be there.

It was 9:00 in the morning, and I was due in court at 10:00 a.m. Aside from the fact that I was in Washington, D.C., I also explained to the court clerk that I had not been notified about the legal action and was not prepared to defend myself. The clerk told me he was sorry, but my attorney had been properly served. Frantically I called Jim Meyerson in New York. Meyerson was furious and immediately called Joe's firm.

Thanks to Jim Meyerson's intercession, the hearing was ultimately postponed and Joe's firm later submitted papers to Judge Curtin that argued that the request for me to pay Taft's court fees was an outrage. Judge Curtin's court asked for a notarized statement of the debts I had incurred in the lawsuit. Over the seven years they had soared to $138,000. Although the most substantial fee—$89,000 to Joe's law firm—was a part of that figure and was contingent on winning the suit, I was still left with the burdensome responsibility of paying for the mounting out-of-pocket costs for the district trial and the attorney fees on appeal. After sending the judge such paperwork, I felt it was unlikely that he would ask me to pay for the court fees of a multimillion dollar company like Taft Broadcasting—especially since I noticed that some of the costs listed included hotel room, toiletries, and drycleaning for Dino Dinovitz incurred while he was appearing at the trial as a witness for the defense.

Once again I found myself waiting for Judge Curtin to make a decision.

After six months had passed and there was still no word from Judge Curtin, I sent him a polite letter. I asked him to please make a decision on the costs.

March 1988

In March 1988, I played back the messages on my telephone answering machine to find that a reporter wanted me to make a comment on Judge Curtin's decision. I returned the reporter's call and found that Judge Curtin was asking that I pay partial court fees for Taft.

"It is a surprising decision," I told the reporter, my voice unsteady, "and not a good message to people who feel they need to take their civil cases to court." It could have a chilling effect on anyone in Judge Curtin's district who felt he or she had been wronged. Can any one person afford the risk of losing in a federal trial, if somewhere down the legal system line, he or she may have to face the ultimate humiliation and hardship of being forced to pay the court fees of the company against whom suit had been brought?

I was shocked at Judge Curtin's ruling. But this time—I knew—it was the end of the road. The case that I thought would never end was finally over.

Chapter 15

Understanding the System

So far the courts have been murky on the issue. "Decisions often have depended on the quirks of one court or judge vs. another," says Kathleen Neville, vice president of Women's Action for Good Employment Standards, a national women's rights organization that tracks cases. "But as more of these cases get into court and employers start discussing them, a clearer picture will emerge."

Wall Street Journal
February 10, 1988

The Dark Side of the Desk

According to an article in the May 21, 1988 issue of the *Washington Post*, after mowing the lawn at his home in Pelham, New York, U.S. District Court Judge Richard J. Daronco was murdered. According to the *Post*, the 56-year-old judge was fatally shot by the father of a woman who had just been informed by Judge Daronco that she had lost her seven-year legal battle regarding her claim of sex harassment/discrimination. After killing Judge Daronco, Carolee Koster's father killed himself. Just like my own, the case I was reading about had begun in 1981.

Carolee Koster claimed in her suit against Chase Manhattan Bank, that she was fired when she ended an affair with her boss. Her boss was a vice president of the bank at the time. I realized the situation that had brought her to court was very different from mine, but the area of law it had encompassed was certainly the same.

In his written decision, Judge Daronco said that Carolee Koster had not convinced the court of the harassment claim and that she had failed to prove that the harassment incidents actually occurred.

There was a photograph showing the smiling face of Carolee's father. The article also shared comments about the judge. "He was a decent human being, everyone liked him," said one source. Twice, claimed the article, Carolee had been offered a substantial settlement but had refused it. I winced. According to the judge's clerk, the judge had wanted the case to be settled. The judge's clerk said Carolee Koster appeared to have been consumed by the case. Her father had put most of his life savings into it.

I couldn't read anymore. Carolee was not the only one who had been swallowed up by her legal battle. Two people had lost their lives because of it.

The System

Tragically, Judge Daronco and Charles Koster are two victims of something we refer to as "the system." Such a horrific and senseless ending to what started out merely as a romantic affair between two people on the job can only leave the rest of us wondering how we can even dare to put our faith in any sort of system. When the actions of people on the job lead down a legal road that ends in murder and suicide, it surely must lead us to question further whether "the system"—or any system—works at all. The justice system is supposed to provide law and order, not provoke people to criminal and violent acts.

After reading the newspaper account about Judge Daronco's murder, I couldn't shake off the feeling I was left with. I was one person who understood what was between the lines in the story; in fact, I think I understood only too well.

It had been just a year since I had received Judge Curtin's original decision. It had only been a few weeks since I had been informed by Judge Curtin that I was to pay Taft's court fees. I was coming to terms with what I had gone through over the years. In a reasonably quiet fashion, I was slowly and carefully putting the pieces of my life back together. Although I had accepted the way things had turned out, my wounds were still fresh, and reading about the tragic ending of a story that had followed the same time line as mine brought everything rushing back to me.

Worst of all, it brought back the haunting question that I thought I had suppressed—the question that pointedly asked *"Why hadn't the system worked?"* Somewhere along the complicated lines of the corporate system, the social system, the legal system, the judicial system, I thought, it should have worked. Why hadn't it?

FINDING ANSWERS THROUGH THE SYSTEM

In all fairness to those who devised it, the so-called system can't be held responsible for everything that goes awry in our society. By the time such civil actions as sexual harassment arrive on the doorsteps of the courts, they often resemble an unidentifiable substance that has been pureed, chopped, and whipped up for years in the powerful, relentless blender called the legal system. It's sometimes hard for the courts to identify just what it is that is standing before them. I felt as though my own case was one huge blob by the time it rolled into federal court. And "the blob" had more of a life, more of an existence, than I had. Somewhere within that mass, my own life and my own singular cause of action had been little particles that had been swallowed up by something larger.

In addition, these sexual harassment suits that appear before the courts are a relatively new species of civil rights action for the system's judges. Sexual harassment is a subjective issue, and most judges simply are not comfortable with their own personal abilities to identify such unclear issues. While corporations are busily drawing lines regarding definitions, so, and somewhat reluctantly, are the courts. Because such uncertainty still exists, many judges fear these cases, some try to ignore them, and others want to make them go away. A Washington, D.C. labor attorney, Allan Seigel, says that the present-day general reaction of the federal courts when they see a sexual harassment suit coming is that they are "mildly antagonist." And, says Seigel about the state courts, they can be viewed as "violently antagonist."

Certainly, those who accompany such cases into court come out worse for the wear. The parties who finally manage to crawl up to the last step of the system are often so wounded from the obstacles they have met on the road to court that they are unable to distinguish which injury hurts them more: the original one or all of the new ones they suffered through along the path to justice. According to Jean Hamilton, a psychiatrist for the Women's Institute for Mental Health, the "second injury," referring to what a victim of sexual harassment faces as he/she goes through the court system, is often more damaging than the original complaint. Because of the sexual nature of the suits, the plaintiffs usually must bear the same scrutiny as rape victims do.

It is no wonder that emotions are high once these impassioned cases get their day in court. Filled with total frustration from their long journey, the parties engage in a heated battle—and that combat becomes the only issue that has any reality to it. To most, winning that battle becomes *everything*. It becomes a matter of life and death.

But instead of vindication, often both defendants and plaintiffs find that no one is able to walk away from court without having suffered great loss, and worse, even more confusion as to who actually won. Like children in a school principal's office after a playground fight, through tears and outbursts of anger and accusations, it is often difficult to uncover who hit who—first. The reason for the squabble is often lost forever in the fury of clenched fists. And often, without clear answers, both children get punished. For the moment, the original cause of the fight seems all but forgotten.

When I lost my case, Thea told me to try and be glad that I won on the issue of sexual harassment. Remember, she said, the judge had found that I had established a prima facie case of quid pro quo sexual harassment. I had trouble clinging to my little prize that showed that I had taken a chance. As at a carnival game, I had been given a pat on the head and a little plastic token and told, "Sorry little girl, maybe next time."

And, of course, there is the issue of the costs of these cases. Companies admit that fighting one sexual harassment case can cost them between $300,000-$500,000—and, that's just for one case. Companies are spending millions of dollars each year defending themselves from claims of sexual harassment.

For those who raise the complaints, the personal costs are even greater. On paper, my own particular case added up to well over six figures, and I could never find any numbers that would adequately reflect the high price of my years of silent emotional pain not to mention the loss of my career. I will always wonder what might have been. I also knew that the case had cost me my personal life. My wish to get married and have children and lead a "normal" life, was something that had to be put on hold for almost a decade. No financial figures can be assigned to show the loss of hope that was crowded out and dreams that had no room to grow.

WHERE DO WE GO FROM HERE?

In order to manage sexual harassment in our society, we need to manage sexual harassment on the job. We need to go right back to the beginning, to where it all starts. There is only one word that can help prevent behavior on the job from leading to costly litigation, job loss, and personal pain to individuals and companies—EDUCATION.

Individuals must be made aware of what the definitions of acceptable workplace behavior are—and this educational process must be continual and constant. The message that sexual harassment is serious needs to be understood by both men and women in the workplace. Once the line between a good working relationship and sexual harassment is crossed, the situation becomes deeply serious.

The educational process in corporate America needs help. According to a recent study of Fortune 500 firms, many corporations are still not responding quickly enough or in proper fashion to eliminate or reduce complaints of sexual harassment. Because of this failure to adequately inform, educate, and enforce, some companies actually do deserve to land in court. A lawsuit is a hard lesson but it does force changes. Once in court is often enough for companies to learn the importance of managing sexual harassment.

Companies also need to communicate better with their employees by providing better avenues for grievance procedures. In addition to having a comprehensive education plan for all employees, the education and training of managers who are positioned to hear grievances needs to be a consistent process. Because top level managers move from company to company at a steady rate, they often are not familiar with or interested in personnel policies found at their new company. They are solely focused on performing their job. It is the responsibility of the companies to educate these managers better.

Men and women make up our workforce—and that is not going to change. Therefore, companies have no choice but to address diligently the challenge of eliminating sexual harassment in the workplace because the issue will never go away, and it is one that companies will undoubtedly always be held responsible for—in some way, whether morally or monetarily. If the moral responsibility doesn't motivate the companies to respond to this issue, then I suspect that the monetary concern will get their attention.

As the U.S. armed forces have seen the number of women members grow over the past ten years, they have had to face and deal with the issue of men and women being together on the job just as corporations have. Perhaps the military services faced the toughest challenge of all when it came to women entering their workforce because it was no secret that that workplace was traditionally designed for men. When women joined the ranks of the military, the entire system needed to adjust—and it needed to adjust in a big way.

According to General Myrna Williamson, the highest ranking woman in the United States Army, "education is everything" in preventing sexual harassment. General Williamson cites three important ingredients in managing sexual harassment: education, engineering and enforcement. She believes that the definitions of behavior must be understood by everyone. Within the first two days after an individual enters the army, that person is informed of the sexual harassment policy. The complaint procedure is available and understood by everyone. And although complaints of sexual harassment are on the rise in the army, General Williamson believes that that is a good sign because it shows belief in the complaint procedure. "It is confidence in the system. They can bring their complaints to someone's attention and believe that they will be dealt with properly."

When a claim of sexual harassment is found valid, says Lt. Colonel Joseph, Chief of the Equal Opportunity Branch, the army trusts its own methods of correction and enforcement. As stated in the policy on equal opportunity and sexual harassment:

> "As we transition into the 21st Century, we must once again reaffirm our sacred commitment to people by insuring that we remain on course in the area of equal opportunity and human relations. This means that all our personnel must feel that the Army is committed to the preservation of their dignity, their upward mobility, and their fair and impartial treatment. In short, we must remain the role model for America. While we can be proud of our past

efforts in these critical areas, it is imperative that we maintain our momentum and remain vigilant and sensitive to the human needs of our personnel. Members of the Total Army will not be discriminated against or sexually harassed. While we are educating those who fail to share these institutional values, and disciplining those who violate applicable laws, each of us must make a personal as well as organizational commitment to eliminate any process, procedure, or system that directly or indirectly abrogates fair treatment, basic human dignity and equal opportunity."

Like the army, major companies recognize the need to insure their employees of the right to work in an offensive-free environment and make such statements within their policy. The Washington law firm of Arent, Fox, Kintner, Plotkin & Kahn recommends the following wording for their clients' corporate policy on sexual harassment:

It is the policy of this company that all of our employees should be able to enjoy a work atmosphere free from all forms of discrimination, including sexual harassment.

Sexual harassment infringes on an employee's right to a comfortable work environment, and is a form of misconduct which undermines the intergrity of the employment relationship. No employee—male or female—should be subjected to unsolicited and unwelcome sexual overtures or conduct, either verbal or physical.

Sexual harassment does not mean occasional compliments of a socially acceptable nature. Sexual harassment refers to conduct which is offensive to the individual, which harms morale, and which interferes with the effectiveness of our business.

Such conduct is prohibited. This includes repeated offensive sexual flirtations, advances, or propositions; continued or repeated verbal abuse of a sexual nature; explicit or degrading verbal comments about another individual or his or her appearance; the display of sexually suggestive pictures or object; or any offensive or abusive physical conduct. It also includes the taking of or the refusal to take any personnel action on the basis of an employee's submission to or refusal of sexual overtures. No employee should so much as imply that an individual's "cooperation" will have any effect on the individual's employment, assignment, compensation, advancement, career development, or any other condition of employment.

The company *will* take immediate disciplinary action against any employee engaging in sexual harassment. Such action may include, depending on the circumstances, suspension, demotion or discharge.

Any questions regarding this policy should be addressed to ________. Any employee who believes that he or she had been the victim of sexual harassment, or who has any knowledge of that kind of behavior, is urged to report such conduct immediately to ________.

THE LEGAL SYSTEM

It is not only individual employees and companies which need to be educated on the issue of sexual harassment in the workplace. There is a crying need in our legal system for more lawyers who understand the complexities of the issue—and there is an even greater need for education of our judges.

During my years in court, it became very clear to me that my problem didn't belong there. Business disputes really should be resolved in the business environment. Even though it ended up being the only place I could take my problem—the courtroom is not the most ideal place to solve an employee/employer dispute. The right place would have been back in Jim Conshafter's office. But, we already know all about that.

Sexual harassment is still a relatively new area of law for attorneys, and it is one that requires a solid level of expertise. Unfortunately, the only way lawyers are going to get better at trying these cases is for them to take on more of them. With each case they learn value lessons that can certainly help their *next* client.

Even more problematical than the limited availability of experienced lawyers is the need for more informed judges, many of whom are wholly unfamiliar with the workplace environment. Because of the subjective issue of sexual harassment, an even more difficult and thoughtful evaluation of the mere nature of the case must be done. Overlooking the fact that I contend that the wrong standard of law was applied to my court claim, I believe that Judge Curtin had two basic problems with my case: He was trying to figure out what sexual harassment is—and what it felt like. It wasn't rape, so what was it? He called what I experienced "disquieting." I believe that was the best he could do as far as describing what he thought sexual harassment must feel like.

Unfortunately, the only way judges like Judge Curtin can become more familiar with the issue of sexual harassment is to hear more cases. I am certain that they will have plenty of chances. Despite the adversity faced by those who risk everything to fight, the number of sexual harassment cases that reach the courts will continue to rise. The working person today, particularly the working woman, is a special breed. She no longer walks away when she feels her own personal rights have been violated. Saying no to sexual harassment is believed to be a right and, in the workplace, it is an important right. As attorney Allan Seigel states, " It is a risk when someone takes a sexual harassment case to court, but ultimately it is the only way to correct a wrong. Over a period of time, the system will improve, it will be a maturation process."

The stand-up and stand-alone approach shown by individuals is suprising to companies and most definitely surprising to the courts. Although fighting sexual harassment is a nasty and terrible business, I know many, many people who, once faced with the prospect of going to court to fight for something they believe is right, would be willing to put their personal lives aside and just, simply go do it.

After all, I did.

Epilogue

The Narrow Path

"I can't tell you just now what the moral of that is, but I shall remember it in a bit."
"Perhaps it hasn't one," Alice ventured to remark.
"Tut, tut, child," said the Duchess. "Everything's got a moral, if only you find it."

Alice's Adventures in Wonderland
Lewis Carroll

Finding a moral to my story was a tough task. In fact, I couldn't find one on my own. It was one of my more philosophical friends who found it for me.

Offering inspiration, my understanding friend quoted something written by Longfellow and told me that the only thing any of us really wants to do with our lives is "make a difference." I wasn't quite convinced that my long and drawn out efforts had somehow managed to make a difference. After all, I had not won my case; I had lost it. How could losing a court case make a bit of difference to someone else?

But he had given me the small hope I had been looking for since the case ended, and I couldn't put what my friend had said out of my mind. Going on with my life would be a lot easier, I thought, if I knew that what I had gone through really had helped someone—anyone—else.

Although I had begun to counsel others in managing sexual harassment even before the verdict in my own court case had been reached, I wasn't sure whether my own work and personal efforts mattered. After all, sexual harassment is an enormous problem. How can one person's lonely efforts and personal experience affect a huge dilemma?

And my journey through the process had been so lonely. So many times I wished that there had been someone else to talk to who had gone through a similar experience. But few had gone as far as I had. There had been no footsteps for me to follow.

I remembered which Longfellow poem my friend was referring to—but I hadn't thought about it in years. I was skeptical that an English poet could possibly have written something in the 1800s that would supply me with a sensible reason for going through all that I had.

I located the poem called "The Psalm of Life," and found the stanza he was referring to:

Lives of great men all remind us
We can make our lives sublime
And departing, leave behind us
Footprints on the sands of time.

Footprints that perhaps another,
Sailing o'er life's solemn main,
A forlorn and shipwrecked brother,
Seeing, shall take heart again.

Okay, I thought desperately. I'll take it.

But if this was to be the moral to my story—what I would cling to, years from now, it would need some contemporary revision. Yes, I had left some footprints—all the way through the federal court system. The fact that they happened to be made by high heels shouldn't disturb Longfellow's original intended message in the least. And I'm sure he meant to mention that the footsteps were for both men and women, not just shipwrecked brothers.

Longfellow made a good point. It is always easier to go some place if you know someone else has been there already—and *survived*, I thought. Narrow paths, after being used by many, become wider and better. Winning or losing my case wasn't so important. What was important was that I had brought the issue of sexual harassment before the public eye. Laws are bettered, policies are developed and strengthened, and people become more educated when they have someone else's experience from which to learn.

Yes, I thought, many important lessons are learned from cases like mine. Already, very recent cases show signs that judges are starting to become more comfortable with this area of law, lawyers are becoming better skilled, and, most important, companies and their employees are acting more responsibly. Even Channel 2.

During the week of July 10, 1989, just a few months before publication of this book, my former employer, Buffalo's Channel 2, ran a three-part special on sexual harassment during its 11 p.m. news broadcast. The series, entitled, "Play or Pay," stressed the seriousness and magnitude of the problem of sexual harassment and spoke of the urgent and critical need for help and assistance for those individuals facing sexual harassment on the job.

Seven years later, Channel 2 and I finally agreed. Take heart.

Kathleen Neville

PUBLISHER'S NOTE

In 1983, Channel 2 was sold by Taft Broadcasting.

In 1984, the small advertising agency where Maria Tucker served as vice president went bankrupt.

In 1986, Sue Pearce, business manager for Channel 2 and the former "impartial internal investigator," was asked to resign from her position.

In 1987, the properties of Taft Broadcasting were sold. The company "Taft Broadcasting" no longer exists as a corporate entity.

In 1989, Sylvester Thomas Cochran "resigned" from his position as local sales manager at Channel 2. Cochran told the press that it was for business reasons.

Dino Dinovitz and Jim Conshafter are continuing their careers in television management at different stations somewhere in the Midwest.

After experiencing the misfortune of two fires in the warehouse, Gary Doebler of Recreational Warehouse left the business of selling discount pools and gas grills.

Appendix A

About the Equal Employment Opportunity Commission

THE EQUAL EMPLOYMENT OPPORTUNITY COMMISSION

The U.S. Equal Employment Opportunity Commission was created by Title VII of the Civil Rights Act of 1964, which prohibits employment discrimination based on race, color, sex, religion or national origin. Since 1979, EEOC also has been responsible for enforcing the Age Discrimination in Employment Act of 1967, which protects employees 40 years of age or older, the Equal Pay

Act of 1963, which protects men and women who perform substantially equal work in the same establishment from sex-based wage discrimination and Section 501 of the Rehabilitation Act of 1973, which prohibits federal sector handicap discrimination.

EEOC also provides oversight and coordination of all federal equal employment opportunity regulations, practices and policies.

The Commission

EEOC has five commissioners and a general counsel appointed by the President and confirmed by the Senate. Commissioners are appointed for five-year staggered terms. The term of the general counsel is four years. The President designates a chairman and a vice chairman. The chairman is the chief executive officer of the Commission. The five-member Commission makes equal employment opportunity policy and approves all litigation. The general counsel is responsible for conducting EEOC enforcement litigation.

Work of the Commission

EEOC staff receive and investigate employment discrimination charges against private employers and state and local governments. If the investigation shows reasonable cause to believe that discrimination occurred, the Commission will begin conciliation efforts. If EEOC is unable to conciliate the charge it will be considered for possible litigation. The Commission's policy is to seek full and effective relief for each and every victim of employment discrimination whether it is sought in court or in conciliation agreements before litigation and to provide remedies designed to correct the sources of discrimination and prevent its recurrence. The Justice Department is the only federal agency which may sue a state or local government for a violation of Title VII. EEOC may sue a state or local government for violations of the ADEA and EPA. If the Commission decides not to litigate a charge, a notice of the right to file a private suit in a federal district court will be given to the charging party.

In the federal government, EEOC staff oversee agencies' affirmative action efforts and their administrative complaints process, administer the complaints hearings program and review final agency decisions on complaints. If that review demonstrates that discrimination has occurred which has not been fully remedied, EEOC may order the agency to provide complete relief.

EEOC'S Mission

The mission of the Commission is to ensure equality of opportunity by vigorously enforcing federal laws prohibiting employment discrimination through investigation, conciliation, litigation, coordination, education and technical assistance.

The Commission's Meetings

In accordance with the Government in the Sunshine Act, meetings of the Commission are open to the public. However, all or part of a meeting may be closed for consideration of matters exempted under the Sunshine Act, such as recommendations for litigation, litigation strategy and other specified matters. For information about Commission meetings, call (202) 634-6748.

Agenda items for Commission meetings are announced

in the Federal Register one week in advance of the meeting.

Headquarters Offices and Their Functions

Audit: Conducts internal and external investigations and audits related to the programs and operation of the Commission.

Communications and Legislative Affairs: Serves as the Commission's primary external communications link with the news media, the U.S. Congress, constituency groups and the public and conducts internal communications.

General Counsel: Recommends and conducts all EEOC litigation in class, systemic and individual cases of discrimination and subpoena enforcement actions. Presents the Commission's views *amicus curiae* in cases in which the Commission is not a party.

Legal Counsel: Serves as principal advisor to the Commission on non-enforcement litigation matters and represents the Commission in defensive litigation and administrative hearings. Develops all policy guidance for Commission consideration and carries out the Commission's leadership and coordination role for the federal government's EEO programs.

Management: Oversees administrative, financial, personnel and management support services. Develops and administers the Commission's budget and is responsible for the Commission's internal EEO program.

Program Operations: Manages, directs and coordinates field office operations and systemic investigations. Develops policy guidance for federal agency affirmative action programs and provides guidance and a hearing program for federal discrimination complaints. Implements the Commission's state and local charge deferral and contracting program and conducts the national EEO survey report program.

Review and Appeals: Decides or recommends decisions to the Commission on appeals from federal agency decisions on EEO complaints or negotiated bargaining agreement grievances where allegations of discrimination are raised and on petitions for review of Merit Systems Protection Board decisions involving allegations of discrimination. Monitors and ensures federal agency compliance with Commission orders regarding remedies on behalf of the complainant. Conducts an outreach program which provides technical assistance, information and training to promote effective use of complaint processing systems and coordination between federal dispute resolution agencies.

Field Operations

EEOC has 23 district, one field, 16 area and 10 local offices. District offices are full service units which investigate charges and systemic cases and conduct litigation. Area offices investigate charges including charges for potential litigation. Local offices investigate charges but forward cases to district offices for litigation development.

EEOC District, Local and Area Offices

Albuquerque, N.M.*
Atlanta, Ga.
Baltimore, Md.
Birmingham, Ala.
Boston, Mass.*
Buffalo, N.Y.**
Charlotte, N.C.
Detroit, Mich.
El Paso, Texas*
Fresno, Calif.**
Greensboro, N.C.**
Greenville, S.C.**
Honolulu, Hawaii**
Houston, Texas

Chicago, Ill.
Cincinnati, Ohio*
Cleveland, Ohio
Dallas, Texas
Denver, Colo.
Indianapolis, Ind.
Jackson, Miss.*
Kansas City, Kan.*
Little Rock, Ark.*
Los Angeles, Calif.

Appendix B

Title VII

An Act

To enforce the constitutional right to vote, to confer jurisdiction upon the district courts of the United States to provide injunctive relief against discrimination in public accommodations, to authorize the Attorney General to institute suits to protect constitutional rights in public facilities and public education, to extend the Commission on Civil Rights, to prevent discrimination in federally assisted programs, to establish a Commission on Equal Employment Opportunity, and for other purposes.

Be it enacted by the Senate and House of Representatives of the United States of America in Congress assembled. That this Act may be cited as the "Civil Rights Act of 1964".

TITLE VII—EQUAL EMPLOYMENT OPPORTUNITY

Definitions

SEC. 701. For the purposes of this Title—

(a) The term "person" includes one or more individuals,

governments, governmental agencies, political subdivisions, labor unions, partnerships, associations, corporations, legal representatives, associations, corporations legal representatives, mutual companies, joint-stock companies, trusts, unincorporated organizations, trustees, trustees in bankruptcy, or receivers.

(b) The term "employer" means a person engaged in an industry affecting commerce who has fifteen or more employees for each working day in each of twenty or more calendar weeks in the current or preceding calendar year, and any agent of such a person, but such term does not include (1) the United States, a corporation wholly owned by the Government of the United States, an Indian tribe, or any department or agency of the District of Columbia subject by statute to procedures of the competitive service (as defined in section 2102 of title 5 of the United States Code), or (2) a bona fide private membership club (other than a labor organization) which is exempt from taxation under section 501(c) of the Internal Revenue Code of 1954, except that during the first year after the date of enactment of the Equal Employment Opportunity Act of 1972, persons having fewer than twenty-five employees (and their agents) shall not be considered employers.

(c) The term "employment agency" means any person regularly undertaking with or without compensation to procure employees for an employer or to procure for employees opportunities to work for an employer and includes an agent of such a person.

(d) The term "labor organization" means a labor organization engaged in an industry affecting commerce, and any agent of such an organization, and includes any organization of any kind, any agency, or employee representation committee, group, association, or plan so engaged in which employees participate and which exists for the purpose, in whole or in part, of dealing with employers concerning grievances, labor disputes, wages, rates of pay, hours, or other terms or conditions of employment, and any conference, general committee, joint or system board, or joint council so engaged which is subordinate to a national or international labor organization.

(e) A labor organization shall be deemed to be engaged in an industry affecting commerce if (1) it maintains or operates a hiring hall or hiring office which procures employees for an employer or procures for employees opportunities to work for an employer, or (2) the number of its members (or, where it is a labor organization composed of other labor organizations or their representatives, if the aggregate number of the members of such other labor organization) is (A) twenty-five or more during the first year after the date of enactment of the Equal Employment Opportunity Act of 1972, or (B) fifteen or more thereafter, and such labor organization—

(1) is the certified representative of employees under the provisions of the National Labor Relations Act, as amended, or the Railway Labor Act, as amended;

(2) although not certified, is a national or international labor organization or a local labor organization recognized or acting as the representative of employees of an employer or employers engaged in an industry affecting commerce; or

(3) has chartered a local labor organization or subsidiary body which is representing or actively seeking to represent employees of employers within the meaning of paragraph (1) or (2); or

(4) has been chartered by a labor organization representing or actively seeking to represent employees within the meaning of paragraph (1) or (2) as the local or subordinate body through which such employees may enjoy mem-

bership or become affiliated with such labor organization; or

(5) is a conference, general committee, joint or system board, or joint council subordinate to a national or international labor organization, which includes a labor organization engaged in an industry affecting commerce within the meaning of any of the preceding paragraphs of this subsection.

(f) The term "employee" means an individual employed by an employer, except that the term 'employee' shall not include any person elected to public office in any State or political subdivision of any State by the qualified voters thereof; or any person chosen by such officer to be on such officer's personal staff, or an appointee on the policymaking level or an immediate adviser with respect to the exercise of the constitutional or legal powers of the office. The exemption set forth in the preceding sentence shall not include employees subject to the civil service laws of a State government, governmental agency or political subdivision.

(g) The term "commerce" means trade, traffic, commerce, transportation, transmission, or communication among the several States: or between a State and any place outside thereof; or within the District of Columbia, or a possession of the United States; or between points in the same State but through a point outside thereof.

(h) The term "industry affecting commerce" means any activity, business, or industry in commerce or in which a labor dispute would hinder or obstruct commerce or the free flow of commerce and includes any activity or industry "affecting commerce" within the meaning of the Labor-Management Reporting and Disclosure Act of 1959, and further includes any governmental industry, business, or activity.

(i) The term "State" includes a State of the United States, the District of Columbia, Puerto Rico, the Virgin Islands, American Samoa, Guam, Wake Island, the Canal Zone, and Outer Continental Shelf lands defined in the Outer Continental Shelf Lands Act.

(j) The term "religion" includes all aspects of religious observance and practice, as well as belief, unless an employer demonstrates that he is unable to reasonably accommodate to an employee's or prospective employee's, religious observance or practice without undue hardship on the conduct of the employer's business.

"(k) The terms, 'because of sex' or 'on the basis of sex' include, but are not limited to, because of or on the basis of pregnancy, childbirth or related medical conditions; and women affected by pregnancy, childbirth or related medical conditions shall be treated the same for all employment-related purposes, including receipt of benefits under fringe benefit programs, as other persons not so affected but similar in their ability or inability to work, and nothing in section 703(h) of this title shall be interpreted to permit otherwise. This subsection shall not require an employer to pay for health insurance benefits for abortion, except where the life of the mother would be endangered if the fetus were carried to term, or except where medical complications have arisen from an abortion: *Provided*, That nothing herein shall preclude an employer from providing abortion benefits or otherwise affect bargaining agreements in regard to abortion."

Exemption

SEC. 702. This title shall not apply to an employer with respect to the employment of aliens outside any State, or to a religious corporation, association, educational institution, or society with respect to the employment of individuals of a particular religion to perform work connected with the carrying on by such corporation, association, educational institution, or society of its activities.

Discrimination Because of Race, Color, Religion, Sex, or National Origin

SEC. 703. (a) It shall be an unlawful employment practice for an employer—

(1) to fail or refuse to hire or to discharge any individual, or otherwise to discriminate against any individual with respect to his compensation, terms, conditions, or privileges of employment, because of such individual's race, color, religion, sex, or national origin; or

(2) To limit, segregate, or classify his employees or applicants for employment in any way which would deprive or tend to deprive any individual of employment opportunities or otherwise adversely affect his status as an employee, because of such individual's race, color, religion, sex, or national origin.

(b) it shall be an unlawful employment practice for an employment agency to fail or refuse to refer for employment, or otherwise to discrimination against, any individual because of his race, color, religion, sex, or national origin, or to classify or refer for employment any individual on the basis of his race, color, religion, sex, or national origin.

(c) It shall be an unlawful employment practice for a labor organization—

(1) to exclude or to expel from its membership, or otherwise to discriminate against any individual because of his race, color, religion, sex, or national origin;

(2) to limit, segregate, or classify its membership, or applicants for membership or to classify or fail or refuse to refer for employment any individual, in any way which would deprive or tend to deprive any individual of employment opportunities, or would limit such employment opportunities or otherwise adversely affect his status as an employee or as an applicant for employment, because of such individual's race, color, religion, sex, or national origin; or

(3) to cause or attempt to cause an employer to discriminate against an individual in violation of this section.

(d) It shall be an unlawful employment practice for any employer, labor organization, or joint labor-management committee controlling apprenticeship or other training or retraining, including on-the-job training programs to discriminate against any individual because of his race, color, religion, sex, or national origin in admission to, or employment in, any program established to provide apprenticeship or other training.

(e) Notwithstanding any other provision of this title, (1) it shall not be an unlawful employment practice for an employer to hire and employ employees, for an employment agency to classify, or refer for employment any individual, for a labor organization to classify its membership or to classify or refer for employment any individual, or for an employer, labor organization, or joint labor-management committee controlling apprenticeship or other training or retraining programs to admit or employ any individual in any such program, on the basis of his religion, sex, or national origin in those certain instances where religion, sex, or national origin is a bona fide occupational qualification reasonably necessary to the normal operation of that particular business or enterprise, and (2) it shall not be an unlawful employment practice for a school, college, university, or other education institution or institution of learning to hire and employ employees of a particular religion if such school, college, university, or other educational institution or institution of learning is, in whole or in substantial part, owned, supported, controlled, or managed by a particular religion or by a particular religious corporation, association, or society, or if the curriculum of such school, college, university, or other educational institution or institution of learning is directed toward the propagation of a particular religion.

(f) As used in this title, the phrase "unlawful employment practice" shall not be deemed to include any action or measure taken by an employer, labor organization, joint labor-management committee, or employment agency with respect to an individual who is a member of the Communist Party of the United States or of any other organization required to register as a Communist-action or Communist-front organization by final order of the Subversive Activities Control Board pursuant to the Subversive Activities Control Act of 1950.

(g) Notwithstanding any other provision of this title, it shall not be an unlawful employment practice for an employer to fail or refuse to hire and employ any individual for any position, for an employer to discharge any individual from any position, or for an employment agency to fail or refuse to refer any individual for employment in any position, or for a labor organization to fail or refuse to refer any individual for employment in any position, if—

(1) the occupancy of such position, or access to the premises in or upon which any part of the duties of such position is performed or is to be performed, is subject to any requirement imposed in the interest of the national security of the United States under any security program in effect pursuant to or administered under any statute of

the United States or any Executive order of the President; and

(2) such individual has not fulfilled or has ceased to fulfill that requirement.

(h) Notwithstanding any other provision of this title, it shall not be an unlawful employment practice for an employer to apply different standards of compensation, or different terms, conditions, or privileges of employment pursuant to a bona fide seniority or merit system, or a system which measures earnings by quantity or quality of production or to employees who work in different locations, provided that such differences are not the result of an intention to discriminate because of race, color, religion, sex, or national origin, or shall it be an unlawful employment practice for an employer to give and to act upon the results of any professionally developed ability test provided that such test, its administration or action upon the results is not designed, intended or used to discriminate because of race, color, religion, sex, or national origin. It shall not be an unlawful employment practice under this title for any employer to differentiate upon the basis of sex in determining the amount of the wages or compensation paid or to be paid to employees of such employer if such differentiation is authorized by the provisions of section 6(d) of the Fair Labor Standards Act of 1938, as amended (29 U.S.C. 206(d)).

(i) Nothing contained in this title shall apply to any business or enterprise on or near an Indian reservation with respect to any publicly announced employment practice of such business or enterprise under which a preferential treatment is given to any individual because he is an Indian living on or near a reservation.

(j) Nothing contained in this title shall be interpreted to require any employer, employment agency, labor organization, or joint labor-management committee subject to this title to grant preferential treatment to any individual or to any group because of the race, color, religion, sex, or national origin of such individual or group on account of an imbalance which may exist with respect to the total number or percentage of persons of any race, color, religion, sex, or national origin employed by any employer, referred or classified for employment by any employment agency or labor organization, admitted to membership or classified by any labor organization, or admitted to, or employed in, any apprenticeship or other training program, in comparison with the total number or percentage of persons of such race, color, religion, sex, or national origin in any community, State, section, or other area, or in the available work force in any community, State, section, or other area.

Other Unlawful Employment Practices

SEC. 704. (a) It shall be an unlawful employment practice for an employer to discriminate against any of his employees or applicants for employment, for an employment agency, or joint labor-management committee controlling apprenticeship or other training or retraining, including on-the-job training programs, to discriminate against any individual, or for a labor organization to discriminate against any member thereof or applicant for membership, because he has opposed any practice made an unlawful employment practice by this title, or because he has made a charge, testified, assisted, or participated in any manner in an investigation, proceeding, or hearing under this title.

(b) It shall be an unlawful employment practice for an employer, labor organization, employment agency, or joint labor-management committee controlling apprenticeship or other training or retraining, including on-the-job training programs, to print or publish or cause to be printed or published any notice or advertisement relating to employment by such an employer or membership in or any classification or referral for employment by such a labor organization, or relating to any classification or referral for employment by such an employment agency, or relating to admission to, or employment in, any program established to provide apprenticeship or other training by such a joint labor-management committee indicating any preference, limitation, specification, or discrimination, based on race, color, religion, sex, or national origin, except that such a notice or advertisement may indicate a preference, limitation, specification, or discrimination based on religion, sex, or national origin when religion, sex, or national origin is a bona fide occupational qualification for employment.

Equal Employment Opportunity Commission

SEC. 705. (a) There is hereby created a Commission to be known as the Equal Employment Opportunity Commission, which shall be composed of five members, not more than three of whom shall be members of the same political party. Members of the Commission shall be appointed by the President by and with the advice and consent of the Senate for a term of five years. Any individual chosen to fill a vacancy shall be appointed only for the unexpired term of the member whom he shall succeed, and all members of the Commission shall continue to serve until their successors are appointed and qualified, except that no such member of the Commission shall continue to serve (1) for more than sixty days when the Congress is in session unless a nomination to fill such vacancy shall have been submitted to the Senate, or (2) after the adjournment sine die of the session of the Senate in which such nomination was submitted. The President shall designate one member to serve as Chairman of the Commission, and one member to serve as Vice Chairman. The Chairman shall be responsible on behalf of the Commission for the administrative operations of the Commission, and except as provided in subsection (b), shall appoint, in accordance with the provisions of title 5, United States Code, governing appointments in the competitive service, such officers, agents, attorneys, hearing examiners, and employees as he deems necessary to assist it in the performance of its functions and to fix their compensation in accordance with the provisions of chapter 51 and subchapter III of chapter 53 of title 5, United States Code, relating to classification and General Schedule pay rates: Provided, That assignment, removal, and compensation of hearing examiners shall be in accordance with sections 3105, 3344, 5362, and 7521 of title 5, United States Code.

(b) (1) There shall be a General Counsel of the Commission appointed by the President, by and with the advice and consent of the Senate, for a term of four years. The General Counsel shall have responsibility for the conduct of litigation as provided in sections 706 and 707 of this title. The General Counsel shall have such other duties as the Commission may prescribe or as may be provided by law and shall concur with the Chairman of the Commission on the appointment and supervision of regional attorneys. The General Counsel of the Commission on the effective date of this Act shall continue in such position and perform the functions specified in this subsection until a successor is appointed and qualified.

(2) Attorneys appointed under this section may, at the

direction of the Commission, appear for and represent the Commission in any case in court, provided that the Attorney General shall conduct all litigation to which the Commission is a party in the Supreme Court pursuant to this title.

(c) A vacancy in the Commission shall not impair the right of the remaining members to exercise all the powers of the Commission and three members thereof shall constitute a quorum.

(d) The Commission shall have an official seal which shall be judicially noticed.

(e) The Commission shall at the close of each fiscal year report to the Congress and to the President concerning the action it has taken; the names, salaries, and duties of all individuals in its employ and the moneys it has disbursed; and shall make such further reports on the cause of and means of eliminating discrimination and such recommendations for further legislation as may appear desirable.

(f) The principal office of the Commission shall be in or near the District of Columbia, but it may meet or exercise any or all its powers at any other place. The Commission may establish such regional or State offices as it deems necessary to accomplish the purpose of this title.

(g) The Commission shall have power—

(1) to cooperate with and, with their consent, utilize regional State, local, and other agencies, both public and private, and individuals;

(2) to pay to witnesses whose depositions are taken or who are summoned before the Commission or any of its agents the same witness and mileage fees as are paid to witnesses in the courts of the United States;

(3) to furnish to persons subject to this title such technical assistance as they may request to further their compliance with this title or an order issued thereunder;

(4) upon the request of (i) any employer, whose employees or some of them, or (ii) any labor organization, whose members or some of them, refuse or threaten to refuse to cooperate in effectuating the provisions of this title, to assist in such effectuation by conciliation or such other remedial action as is provided by this title;

(5) to make such technical studies as are appropriate to effectuate the purposes and policies of this title and to make the results of such studies available to the public;

(6) to intervene in a civil action brought under section 706 by an aggrieved party against a respondent other than a government, governmental agency, or political subdivision.

(h) The Commission shall, in any of its educational or promotional activities, cooperate with other departments and agencies in the performance of such educational and promotional activities.

(i) All officers, agents, attorneys, and employees of the Commission shall be subject to the provisions of section 9 of the Act of August 2, 1939, as amended (the Hatch Act), notwithstanding any exemption contained in such section.

Prevention of Unlawful Employment Practices

SEC. 706. (a) The Commission is empowered, as hereinafter provided, to prevent any person from engaging in any unlawful employment practice as set forth in section 703 or 704 of this title.

(b) Whenever a charge is filed by or on behalf of a person claiming to be aggrieved, or by a member of the Commission, alleging that an employer, employment agency, labor organization, or joint labor-management committee controlling apprenticeship or other training or retraining, including on-the-job training programs, has engaged in an unlawful employment practice, the Commission shall serve a notice of the charge (including the date, place and circumstances of the alleged unlawful employment practice) on such employer, employment agency, labor organization, or joint labor-management committee (hereinafter referred to as the "respondent") within ten days, and shall make an investigation thereof. Charges shall be in writing under oath or affirmation and shall contain such information and be in such form as the Commission requires. Charges shall not be made public by the Commission. If the Commission determines after such investigation that there is not reasonable cause to believe that the charge is true, it shall dismiss the charge and promptly notify the person claiming to be aggrieved and the respondent of its action. In determining whether reasonable cause exists, the Commission shall accord substantial weight to final findings and orders made by State or local authorities in proceedings commenced under State or local law pursuant to the requirements of subsections (c) and (d). If the Commission determines after such investigation that there is reasonable cause to believe that the charge is true, the Commission shall endeavor to eliminate any such alleged unlawful employment practice by informal methods of conference, conciliation, and persuasion. Nothing said or done during and as a part of such informal endeavors may be made public by the Commission, its officers or employees, or used as evidence in a subsequent proceeding without the written consent of the persons concerned. Any person who makes public information in violation of this subsection shall be fined not more than $1,000 or imprisoned for not more than one year, or both. The Commission shall make its determination on reasonable cause as promptly as possible and, so far as practicable, not later than one hundred and twenty days from the filing of the charge or, where applicable under subsection (c) or (d) from the date upon which the Commission is authorized to take action with respect to the charge.

(c) In the case of an alleged unlawful employment practice occurring in a State, or political subdivision of a State, which has a State or local law prohibiting the unlawful employment practice alleged and establishing or authorizing a State or local authority to grant or seek relief from such practice or to institute criminal proceedings with respect thereto upon receiving notice thereof, no charge may be filed under subsection (a) by the person aggrieved before the expiration of sixty days after proceedings have been commenced under the state or local law, unless such proceedings have been earlier terminated, provided that such sixty-day period shall be extended to one hundred and twenty days during the first year after the effective date of such State or local law. If any requirement for the commencement of such proceedings is imposed by a State or local authority other than a requirement of the filing of a written and signed statement of the facts upon which the proceeding is based, the proceeding shall be deemed to have been commenced for the purposes of this subsection at the time such statement is sent by registered mail to the appropriate State or local authority.

(d) In the case of any charge filed by a member of the Commission alleging an unlawful employment practice occurring in a State or political subdivision of a State which has a State or local law prohibiting the practice alleged and establishing or authorizing a State or local authority to grant or seek relief from such practice or to institute criminal proceedings with respect thereto upon receiving notice thereof, the Commission shall, before taking any action with respect to such charge, notify the appropriate State or local officials and, upon request, afford them a reasonable time, but not less than sixty days (provided that such sixty-day period shall be extended to one hundred and twenty days during the first year after the effective date of such State or local law), unless a shorter period is requested, to act under such State or local law to remedy the practice alleged.

(e) A charge under this section shall be filed within one hundred and eighty days after the alleged unlawful employment practice occurred and notice of the charge (including the date, place and circumstances of the alleged unlawful employment practice) shall be served upon the person against whom such charge is made within ten days thereafter, except that in a case of an unlawful employment practice with respect to which the person aggrieved has initially instituted proceedings with a State or local agency with authority to grant or seek relief from such practice or to institute criminal proceedings with respect thereto upon receiving notice thereof, such charge shall be filed by or on behalf of the person aggrieved within three hundred days after the alleged unlawful employment practice occurred, or within thirty days after receiving notice that the State or local agency has terminated the proceedings under the State or local law, whichever is earlier, and a copy of such charge shall be filed by the Commission with the State or local agency.

(f) (1) If within thirty days after a charge is filed with the Commission or within the thirty days after expiration of any period of reference under subsection (c) or (d), the Commission has been unable to secure from the respondent a conciliation agreement acceptable to the Commission, the Commission may bring a civil action against any respondent not a government, governmental agency, or political subdivision named in the charge. In the case of a respondent which is a government, governmental agency, or political subdivision, if the Commission has been unable to secure from the respondent a conciliation agreement acceptable to the Commission, the Commission shall take no further action and shall refer the case to the Attorney General who may bring a civil action against such respondent in the appropriate United States district court. The person or persons aggrieved shall have the right to intervene in a civil action brought by the Commission or the Attorney General in a case involving a government, governmental agency, or political subdivision. If a charge filed with the Commission pursuant to subsection (b) is dismissed by the Commission, or if within one hundred and eighty days from the filing of such charge or the expiration of any period of reference under subsection (c) or (d), whichever is later, the Commission has not filed a civil action under this section or the Attorney General has notified a civil action in a case involving a government, governmental agency, or political subdivision, or the Commission has not entered into a conciliation agreement to which the person aggrieved is a party, the Commission, or the Attorney General in a case involving a government, governmental agency, or political subdivision, shall so notify the person aggrieved and within ninety days after the giving of such notice a civil action may be brought against the respondent named in the charge (A) by the person claiming to be aggrieved, or (B) if such charge was filed by a member of the Commission, by any person whom the charge alleges was aggrieved by the alleged unlawful employment practice. Upon application by the complainant and in such circumstances as the court may deem just, the court may appoint an attorney for such complainant and may authorize the commencement of the action without the payment of fees, costs, or security. Upon timely application, the court may, in its discretion, permit the Commission, or the Attorney General in a case involving a government, governmental agency, or political subdivision, to intervene in such civil action upon certification that the case is of general public importance. Upon request, the court may, in its discretion, stay further proceedings for not more than sixty days pending the termination of State or local proceedings described in subsections (c) or (d) of this section or further efforts of the Commission to obtain voluntary compliance.

(2) Whenever a charge is filed with the Commission and the Commission concludes on the basis of a preliminary investigation that prompt judicial action is necessary to carry out the purposes of this Act, the Commission, or the Attorney General in a case involving a government, governmental agency, or political subdivision, may bring an action for appropriate temporary or preliminary relief pending final disposition of such charge. Any temporary restraining order or other order granting preliminary or temporary relief shall be issued in accordance with rule 65 of the Federal Rules of Civil Procedure. It shall be the duty of a court having jurisdiction over proceedings under this section to assign cases for hearing at the earliest practicable date and to cause such cases to be in every way expedited.

(3) Each United States district court and each United States court of a place subject to the jurisdiction of the United States shall have jurisdiction of actions brought under this title. Such an action may be brought in any judicial district in the State in which the unlawful employment practice is alleged to have been committed, in the judicial district in which the employment records relevant to such practice are maintained and administered, or in the judicial district in which the aggrieved person would

have worked but for the alleged unlawful employment practice, but if the respondent is not found within any such district, such an action may be brought within the judicial district in which the respondent has his principal office. For purposes of sections 1404 and 1406 of title 28 of the United States Code, the judicial district in which the respondent has his principal office shall in all cases be considered a district in which the action might have been brought.

(4) It shall be the duty of the chief judge of the district (or in his absence, the acting chief judge) in which the case is pending immediately to designate a judge in such district to hear and determine the case. In the event that no judge in the district is available to hear and determine the case, the chief judge of the district, or the acting chief judge, as the case may be, shall certify this face to the chief judge of the circuit (or in his absence, the acting chief judge) who shall then designate a district or circuit judge of the circuit to hear and determine the case.

(5) It shall be the duty of the judge designated pursuant to this subsection to assign the case for hearing at the earliest practicable date and to cause the case to be in every way expedited. If such judge has not scheduled the case for trial within one hundred and twenty days after issue has been joined, that judge may appoint a master pursuant to rule 53 of the Federal Rules of Civil Procedure.

(g) If the court finds that the respondent has intentionally engaged in or is intentionally engaging in an unlawful employment practice charged in the complaint, the court may enjoin the respondent from engaging in such unlawful employment practice, and order such affirmative action as may be appropriate, which may include, but is not limited to, reinstatement or hiring of employees, with or without back pay (payable by the employer, employment agency, or labor organization, as the case may be, responsible for the unlawful employment practice), or any other equitable relief as the court deems appropriate. Back pay liability shall not accrue from a date more than two years prior to the filing of a charge with the Commission. Interim earnings or amounts earnable with reasonable diligence by the person or persons discriminated against shall operate to reduce the back pay otherwise allowable. No order of the court shall require the admission or reinstatement of an individual as a member of a union, or the hiring, reinstatement, or promotion of an individual as an employee, or the payment to him of any back pay, if such individual was refused admission, suspended, or expelled, or was refused employment or advancement or was suspended or discharged for any reason other than discrimination on account of race, color, religion, sex, or national origin or in violation of section 704(a).

(h) The provisions of the Act entitled "An Act to amend the Judicial Code and to define and limit the jurisdiction of courts sitting in equity, and for other purposes," approved March 23, 1932 (29 U.S.C. 101-115), shall not apply with respect to civil actions brought under this section.

(i) In any case in which an employer, employment agency, or labor organization fails to comply with an order of a court issued in civil action brought under this section, the Commission may commence proceedings to compel compliance with such order.

(j) Any civil action brought under this section and any proceedings brought under subsection (i) shall be subject to appeal as provided in sections 1291 and 1292, title 28, United States Code.

(k) In any action or proceeding under this title the court, in its discretion, may allow the prevailing party, other than the Commission or the United States, a reasonable attorney's fee as part of the costs, and the Commission and the United States shall be/liable for costs the same as a private person.

SEC 707.

(a) Whenever the Attorney General has reasonable cause to believe that any person or group of persons is engaged in a pattern or practice of resistance to the full enjoyment of any of the rights secured by this title, and that the pattern or practice is of such a nature and is intended to deny the full exercise of the rights herein described, the Attorney General may bring a civil action in the appropriate district court of the United States by filing with it a complaint (1) signed by him (or in his absence the Acting Attorney General), (2) setting forth facts pertaining to such pattern or practice, and (3) requesting such relief, including an application for a permanent or temporary injunction, restraining order or other order against the person or persons responsible for such pattern or practice, as he deems necessary to insure the full enjoyment of the rights herein described.

(b) The district courts of the United States shall have and shall exercise jurisdiction of proceedings instituted pursuant to this section, and in any such proceeding the Attorney General may file with the clerk of such court a request that a court of three judges be convened to hear and determine the case. Such request by the Attorney General shall be accompanied by a certificate that, in his opinion, the case is of general public importance. A copy of the certificate and request for a three-judge court shall be immediately furnished by such clerk to the chief judge of the circuit (or in his absence, the presiding circuit judge of the circuit) in which the case is pending. Upon receipt of such request it shall be the duty of the chief judge of the circuit or the presiding circuit judge, as the case may be, to designate immediately three judges in such circuit, of whom at least one shall be a circuit judge and another of whom shall be a district judge of the court in which the proceeding was instituted, to hear and determine such case, and it shall be the duty of the judges so designated to assign the case for hearing at the earliest practicable date, to participate in the hearing and determination therefor, and to cause the case to be in every way expedited. An appeal from the final judgement of such court will lie to the Supreme Court.

In the event the Attorney General fails to file such a request in any such proceeding, it shall be the duty of the chief judge of the district (or in his absence, the acting chief judge) in which the case is pending immediately to designate a judge in such district to hear and determine the case. In the event that no judge in the district is available to hear and determine the case, the chief judge of the district or the acting chief judge, as the case may be, shall certify this fact to the chief judge of the circuit (or in his absence, the acting chief judge) who shall then designate a district or circuit judge of the circuit to hear and determine the case.

It shall be the duty of the judge designated pursuant to this section to assign the case for hearing at the earliest practicable date and to cause the case to be in every way expedited.

(c) Effective two years after the date of enactment of the Equal Employment Opportunity Act of 1972, the functions of the Attorney General under this section shall be transferred to the Commission, together with such personnel, property, records, and unexpended balances of appropriations, allocations, and other funds employed, used, held, available, or to be made available in connection with such functions unless the President submits, and neither House of Congress vetoes, a reorganization plan pursuant to chapter 9, of title 5, United States Code, inconsistent with the provisions of this subsection. The Commission shall carry out such functions in accordance with subsections (d) and (e) of this section.

(d) Upon the transfer of functions provided for in subsection (c) of this section, in all suits commenced pursuant to this section prior to the date of such transfer, proceedings shall continue without abatement, all court orders and decrees shall remain in effect, and the Commission shall be substituted as a party for the United States of America, the Attorney General, or the Acting Attorney General, as appropriate.

(e) Subsequent to the date of enactment of the Equal Employment Opportunity Act of 1972, the Commission shall have authority to investigate and act on a charge of a pattern or practice of discrimination, whether filed by or on behalf of a person claiming to be aggrieved or by a member of the Commission. All such actions shall be conducted in accordance with the procedures set forth in section 706 of this Act.

Effect on State Laws

SEC. 708. Nothing in this title shall be deemed to exempt or relieve any person from any liability, duty, penalty, or punishment provided by any present or future law of any State or political subdivision of a State, other than any such law which purports to require or permit the doing of any act which would be an unlawful employment practice under this title.

Investigations, Inspections, Records, State Agencies

SEC. 709. (a) In connection with any investigation of a charge filed under section 706, the Commission or its designated representative shall at all reasonable times have access to, for the purposes of examination, and the right to copy and evidence of any person being investigated or proceeded against that relates to unlawful employment practices covered by this title and is relevant to the charge under investigation.

(b) The Commission may cooperate with State and local agencies charged with the administration of State fair employment practices laws and, with the consent of such agencies, may, for the purpose of carrying out its functions and duties under this title and within the limitation of funds appropriated specifically for such purpose, engage in and contribute to the cost of research and other projects of mutual interest undertaken by such agencies, and utilize the services of such agencies and their employees, and, notwithstanding any other provision of law, pay by advance or reimbursement such agencies and their employees for services rendered to assist the Commission in carrying out this title. In furtherance of such cooperative efforts, the Commission may enter into written agreements with such State or local agencies and such agreements may include provisions under which the Commission shall refrain from processing a charge in any cases or class of cases specified in such agreements or under which the Commission shall relieve any person or class of persons in such State or locality from requirements imposed under this section. The Commission shall rescind any such agreement whenever it determines that the agreement no longer serves the interest of effective enforcement of this title.

(c) Every employer, employment agency, and labor organization subject to this title shall (1) make and keep such records relevant to the determinations of whether unlawful employment practices have been or are being committed, (2) preserve such records for such periods, and (3) make such reports therefrom, as the Commission shall prescribe by regulation or order, after public hearing, as reasonable, necessary, or appropriate for the enforcement of this title or the regulations or orders thereunder. The Commission shall, by regulation, require each employer, labor organization, and joint labor-management committee subject to this title which controls an apprenticeship or other training program to maintain such records as are reasonably necessary to carry out the purpose of this title, including, but not limited to, a list of applicants who wish to participate in such program, including the chronological order in which applications were received, and to furnish to the Commission upon request, a detailed description of the manner in which persons are selected to participate in the apprenticeship or other training program. Any employer, employment agency, labor organization, or joint labor-management committee which believes that the application to it of any regulation or order issued under this section would result in undue hardship may apply to the Commission for an exemption from the application of such regulation or order, and, if such application for an exemption is denied, bring a civil action in the United States district court for the district where such records are kept. If the Commission or the court, as the case may be, finds that the application of the regulation or order to the employer, employment agency, or labor organization in question would impose an undue hardship, the Commission or the court, as the case may be, may grant appropriate relief. If any person required to comply with the provisions of this subsection fails or refuses to do so, the United States district court for the district in which such person is found, resides, or transacts business, shall, upon application of the Commission, or the Attorney General in a case involving a government, governmental agency or political subdivision, have jurisdiction to issue to such person an order requiring him to comply.

(d) In prescribing requirements pursuant to subsection (c) of this section, the Commission shall consult with other interested State and Federal agencies and shall endeavor to coordinate its requirements with those adopted by such agencies. The Commission shall furnish upon request and without cost to any State or local agency, charged with the administration of a fair employment practice law information obtained pursuant to subsection (c) of this section from any employer, employment agency, labor organization, or joint labor—management committee subject to the jurisdiction of such agency. Such information shall be furnished on condition that it not be made public by the recipient agency prior to the institution of a proceeding under State or local law involving such information. If this condition is violated by a recipient agency, the Commission may decline to honor subsequent requests pursuant to this subsection.

(e) It shall be unlawful for any officer or employee of the Commission to make public in any manner whatever any information obtained by the Commission pursuant to its authority under this section prior to the institution of any proceeding under this title involving such information. Any officer or employee of the Commission who shall make public in any manner whatever any information in violation of this subsection shall be guilty of a misdemeanor and upon conviction thereof, shall be fined not more than $1,000, or imprisoned not more than one year.

Investigatory Powers

SEC. 710. For the purpose of all hearings and investigations conducted by the Commission or its duly authorized agents or agencies, section 11 of the National Labor Relations Act (49 Stat. 455; 29 U.S.C. 161) shall apply.

Notices to be Posted

SEC. 711. (a) Every employer, employment agency, and labor organization, as the case may be, shall post and keep posted in conspicuous places upon its premises where notices to employees, applicants for employment, and members are customarily posted a notice to be prepared or approved by the Commission setting forth excerpts from, or summaries of, the pertinent provisions of this title and information pertinent to the filing of a complaint.

(b) A willful violation of this section shall be punishable by a fine of not more than $100 for each separate offense.

Veterans' Preference

SEC. 712. Nothing contained in this title shall be construed to repeal or modify any Federal, State, territorial, or local law creating special rights or preference for veterans.

Rules and Regulations

SEC. 713. (a) The Commission shall have authority from time to time to issue, amend, or rescind suitable procedural regulations to carry out the provisions of this title.

Regulations issued under the section shall be in conformity with the standards and limitations of the Administrative Procedure Act.

(b) In any action or proceeding based on any alleged unlawful employment practice, no person shall be subject to any liability or punishment for or on account of (1) the commission by such person of an unlawful employment practice if he pleads and proves that the act or omission complained of was in good faith, in conformity with, and in reliance on any written interpretation or opinion of the Commission, or (2) the failure of such person to publish and file any information required by any provision of this title if he pleads and proves that he failed to publish and file such information in good faith, in conformity with the instructions of the Commission issued under this title regarding the filing of such information. Such a defense, if established, shall be a bar to the action or proceeding, notwithstanding that (A) after such act or omission, such interpretation or opinion is modified or rescinded or is determined by judicial authority to be invalid or of no legal effect, or (B) after publishing or filing the description and annual reports, such publication or filing is determined by judicial authority not to be in conformity with the requirements of this title.

Forcibly Resisting the Commission or its Representatives

SEC. 714. The provisions of sections 111 and 1114 title 18, United States Code, shall apply to officers, agents, and employees of the Commission in the performance of their official duties. Notwithstanding the provisions of sections 111 and 1114 of title 18, United States Code, whoever in violation of the provisions of section 1114 of such title kills a person while engaged in or on account of the performance of his official functions under this Act shall be punished by imprisonment for any term of years or for life.

Transfer of Authority

Administration of the duties of the Equal Employment Opportunity Coordinating Council was transferred to the Equal Employment Opportunity Commission effective July 1, 1978, under the President's Reorganization Plan No. 1 of 1978.

Equal Employment Opportunity Coordinating Council

SEC. 715. There shall be established an Equal Employment Opportunity Coordinating Council (herein after referred to in this section as the Council) composed of the Secretary of Labor, the Chairman of the Equal Employment Opportunity Commission, the Attorney General, the Chairman of the United States Civil Service Commission, and the Chairman of the United States Civil Rights Commission, or their respective delegates. The Council shall have the responsibility for developing and implementing agreements, policies and practices designed to maximize effort, promote efficiency, and eliminate conflict, competition, duplication and inconsistency among the operations, functions and jurisdictions of the various departments, agencies and branches of the Federal government responsible for the implementation and enforcement of equal employment opportunity legislation, orders, and policies. On or before July 1 of each year, the Council shall transmit to the President and to the Congress a report of its activities, together with such recommendations for legislative or administrative changes as it concludes are desirable to further promote the purposes of this section.

Effective Date

SEC. 716. (a) This title shall become effective one year after the date of its enactment.

(b) Notwithstanding subsection (a), sections of this title other than sections 703, 704, 706, and 707 shall become effective immediately.

(c) The President shall, as soon as feasible after the enactment of this title, convene one or more conferences for the purpose of enabling the leaders of groups whose members will be affected by this title to become familiar with the rights afforded and obligations imposed by its provisions, and for the purpose of making plans which will result in the fair and effective administration of this title when all of its provisions become effective. The President shall invite the participation in such conference or conferences of (1) the members of the President's Committee on Equal Employment Opportunity, (2) the members of the Commission on Civil Rights, (3) representatives of State and local agencies engaged in furthering equal employment opportunity, (4) representatives of private agencies engaged in furthering equal employment opportunity, and (5) representatives of employers, labor organizations, and employment agencies who will be subject to this title.

Transfer of Authority

Enforcement of Section 717 was transferred to the Equal Employment Opportunity Commission from the Civil Service Commission (Office of Personnel Management) effective Janu-

ary 1, 1979 under the President's Reorganization Plan No. 1 of 1978.

Nondiscrimination in Federal Government Employment

SEC. 717. (a) All personnel actions affecting employees or applicants for employment (except with regard to aliens employed outside the limits of the United States) in military departments as defined in section 102 of title 5, United States Code, in executive agencies (other than the General Accounting Office) as defined in section 105 of title 5, United States Code (including employees and applicants for employment who are paid from nonappropriated funds), in the United States Postal Service and the Postal Rate Commission, in those units of the Government of the District of Columbia having positions in the competitive service, and in those units of the legislative and judicial branches of the Federal Government having positions in the competitive service, and in the Library of Congress shall be made free from any discrimination based on race, color, religion, sex, or national origin.

(b) Except as otherwise provided in this subsection, the Civil Service Commission shall have authority to enforce the provisions of subsection (a) through appropriate remedies, including reinstatement or hiring of employees with or without back pay, as will effectuate the policies of this section, and shall issue such rules, regulations, orders, and instructions as it deems necessary and appropriate to carry out its responsibilities under this section. The Civil Service Commission shall—

(1) be responsible for the annual review and approval of a national and regional equal employment opportunity

plan which each department and agency and each appropriate unit referred to in subsection (a) of this section shall submit in order to maintain an affirmative program of equal employment opportunity for all such employees and applicants for employment;

(2) be responsible for the review and evaluation of the operation of all agency equal employment opportunity programs, periodically obtaining and publishing (on at least a semiannual basis) progress reports from each such department, agency or unit; and

(3) consult with and solicit the recommendations of interested individuals, groups, and organizations relating to equal employment opportunity.

The head of each such department, agency, or unit shall comply with such rules, regulations, orders, and instructions which shall include a provision that an employee or applicant for employment shall be notified of any final action taken on any complaint of discrimination filed by him thereunder. The plan submitted by each department, agency, and unit shall include, but not be limited to—

(1) provision for the establishment of training and education programs designed to provide a maximum opportunity for employees to advance so as to perform at their highest potential; and

(2) a description of the qualifications in terms of training and experience relating to equal employment opportunity for the principal and operating officials of each such department, agency, or unit responsible for carrying out the equal employment opportunity program and of the allocation of personnel and resources proposed by such department, agency, or unit to carry out its equal employment opportunity program.

With respect to employment in the Library of Congress, authorities granted in this subsection to the Civil Service

Commission shall be exercised by the Librarian of Congress.

(c) Within thirty days of receipt of notice of final action taken by a department, agency, or unit referred to in subsection 717(a), or by the Civil Service Commission upon an appeal from a decision or order of such department, agency, or unit on a complaint of discrimination based on race, color, religion, sex, or national origin, brought pursuant to subsection (a) of this section, Executive Order 11478 or any succeeding Executive orders, or after one hundred and eighty days from the filing of the initial charge with the department, agency, or unit or with the Civil Service Commission on appeal from a decision or order of such department, agency, or unit until such time as final action may be taken by a department, agency, or unit, an employee or applicant for employment, if aggrieved by the final disposition of his complaint, or by the failure to take final action on his complaint, may file a civil action as provided in section 706, in which civil action the head of the department, agency, or unit, as appropriate, shall be the defendant.

(d) The provisions of section 706(f) through (k), as applicable, shall govern civil actions brought hereunder.

(e) Nothing contained in this Act shall relieve any Government agency or official of its or his primary responsibility to assure nondiscrimination in employment as required by the Constitution and statutes or of its or his responsibilities under Executive Order 11478 relating to equal employment opportunity in the Federal Government.

Special Provisions with Respect to Denial, Termination, and Suspension of Government Contracts

SEC. 718. No Government contract, or portion thereof,

with any employer, shall be denied, withheld, terminated, or suspended, by any agency or officer of the United States under any equal employment opportunity law or order, where such employer has an affirmative action plan which has previously been accepted by the Government for the same facility within the past twelve months without first according such employer full hearing and adjudication under the provisions of title 5, United States Code, section 554, and the following pertinent sections: Provided, That if such employer has deviated substantially from such previously agreed to affirmative action plan, this section shall not apply: Provided further, That for the purposes of this section an affirmative action plan shall be deemed to have been accepted by the Government at the time the appropriate compliance agency has accepted such plan unless within forty-five days thereafter the Office of Federal Contract Compliance has disapproved such plan.

FURTHER EXPLANATION OF TITLE VII

Employment discrimination based on race, color, religion, sex or national origin is prohibited by Title VII of the Civil Rights Act of 1964.

Title VII covers private employers, state and local governments, and educational institutions that have 15 or more employees. The federal government, private and public employment agencies, labor organizations and joint labor-management committees for apprenticeship and training also must abide by the law.

It is illegal under Title VII to discriminate in:

- hiring and firing
- compensation, assignment or classification of

employees

- transfer, promotion, layoff or recall
- job advertisements
- recruitment
- testing
- use of company facilities
- training and apprenticeship programs
- fringe benefits
- pay, retirement plans and disability leave
- other terms and conditions of employment.

Under the law, pregnancy, childbirth and related medical conditions must be treated the same as any other temporary medical disability.

Title VII prohibits retaliation against a person who files a charge of discrimination, participates in an investigation or opposes an unlawful employment practice.

Employment agencies cannot discriminate in receiving, classifying or referring applications for employment or in their job advertisements.

Labor unions cannot discriminate in accepting applications for membership, classifying members, referrals, training and apprenticeship programs or job advertisements. It is illegal for a labor union to cause or try to cause an employer to discriminate. It is also illegal to cause or try to cause a union to discriminate.

The Immigration Reform and Control Act of 1986 requires employers to prove all employees hired after Nov. 6, 1986, are legally authorized to work in the United States. An employer who single out individuals or a particular national origin or individuals who appear to be or sound foreign to provide employment verification may have violated both the Immigration Act and Title VII.

Citizenship requirements, preferences or a rule requiring employees to be fluent in English or speak only English at work may be unlawful if they disadvantage individuals of a particular national origin and are not justified by business necessity. For further information about employment rights and responsibilities under the Immigration Reform and Control Act, call the Office of Special Counsel for Immigration-Related Unfair Employment Practices toll free at 800-255-7688.

How to File a Charge

To file a charge of employment discrimination, contact the nearest EEOC field office. If there is not an EEOC office in the immediate area, call toll free 800-USA-EEOC for more information.

A charge of discrimination can be filed by or on behalf of an individual or group. Charges must be filed within 180 days of the alleged discriminatory act. In some states with Fair Employment Practices Agencies, charges may be filed up to 300 days after the act, but it is advisable to contact EEOC promptly when discrimination is suspected.

Federal employees or applicants must file complaints of discrimination with the concerned agency within 30 days of the alleged discriminatory act.

Remedies for Violations of Title VII

The Commission's policy is to seek full and effective relief for each and every victim of employment discrimination, whether it is sought in court or in conciliation agreements reached before litigation. Remedies are tailored to the circumstances. Remedies may include:

- Posting a notice to all employees advising them of their rights under the laws EEOC enforces and their right to be free from retaliation;
- Corrective, curative or preventive actions taken to cure or correct the source of the identified discrimination and minimize the chance of its recurrence;
- Nondiscriminatory placement to the position the victim would have occupied if the discrimination had not occurred, or to a substantially equivalent position;
- Backpay or lost benefits or both;
- Stopping the specific discriminatory practices involved in the case;
- Attorney's fees and court costs.

Enforcement

After a charge is filed, it is investigated by an EEOC investigator. If the investigation shows that there is reasonable cause to believe that discrimination has occurred, the Commission will notify the charging party and the employer of this decision and will begin conciliation efforts.

If the investigation concludes that there is no reasonable cause to believe that discrimination has occurred, the Commission will notify both parties of that decision. Charging parties have the right to request that EEOC headquarters in Washington, D.C., review the field office's decision. Charging parties also will be notified of the right to file a private lawsuit.

If the EEOC finds that there is reasonable cause to believe that discrimination occurred and is unable to conciliate the charge, it will be considered for possible litigation. If the Commission decides not to litigate the case, notice of the right to file a private suit in federal district court will be given.

Additional Information

If you need further information, you may call EEOC toll free on 800-USA-EEOC. EEOC's TDD number for the hearing impaired is (202) 634-7057.

The information in this pamphlet is intended as a general overview and does not carry the force of a legal opinion.

This brochure is available, upon request, in large print, Braille or on tape by writing to the Office of Communications and Legislative Affairs, EEOC, Washington, D.C. 20507.

Material contained in this publication is in the public domain and may be reproduced, fully or partially, without the permission of the federal government.

EEOC enforces Title VII of the Civil Rights Act of 1964, the Age Discrimination in Employment Act of 1967, the Equal Pay Act of 1963 and Section 501 of the Rehabilitation Act of 1973. The text of the laws is contained in the booklet "Laws Enforced by EEOC", available by writing the Office of Communications and Legislative Affairs, EEOC, Washington, D.C. 20507.

Office of Communications and Legislative Affairs
October 1988

Appendix C

Filing A Charge

If you believe that you have been discriminated against by an employer, a labor union or an employment agency when applying for a job or on your job in the terms or conditions of your employment because of race, color, sex, religion, national origin or age, you may file a charge of discrimination against the employer, labor union or employment agency.

In pursuing its mission of eradicating discrimination in the workplace, the Commission intends that its enforcement be predictable, provide effective relief for those affected by discrimination, allow remedies designed to correct the sources of discrimination and prevent its recurrence.

Charges/complaints of employment discrimination may be filed at any field office of the U.S. Equal Employment Opportunity Commission (EEOC). Field offices are located in 48 cities throughout the United States and are listed in most local phone directories under U.S. Government.

EEOC enforces Title VII of the Civil Rights Act of 1964, as amended, the Age Discrimination in Employment Act (ADEA) of 1967, as amended, the Equal Pay Act (EPA) of 1963 and Section 501 of the Rehabilitation Act of 1973, as amended.

The law prohibits discrimination by employers, unions and employment agencies. Throughout the rest of this appendix, however, for the sake of simplicity, reference will be made only to employers. Also, this does not deal with job discrimination against federal employees, or applicants for federal employment, who must file their charges with the allegedly discriminating agency.

FILING YOUR EMPLOYMENT DISCRIMINATION CHARGE

Under Title VII—

(race, color, sex, religion or national origin)

In many places, you must file an employment discrimination charge within 180 days of the alleged discriminatory act. Where there is a State or Local Fair Employment Practices Agency in your area, you generally have up to 240 days, and in some cases up to 300 days, to file your charge with EEOC, but you should check with the Commission. If your charge is not filed on time, EEOC may not be able to investigate it, and you may not be able to secure any relief.

You may file your charge either in person, by mail or by

telephone. However, most people prefer to come into an EEOC office.

The Intake Interview

You will be interviewed by an Equal Opportunity Specialist (EOS). During your initial contact with EEOC, you will be:

- Asked to complete a questionnaire that asks for information such as the name, address and telephone number of your employer, or the place you applied for a job, the name of your supervisor, the date that the alleged discrimination occurred and the nature of the discrimination.
- Interviewed about your allegations so that the charge may be properly written.
- Asked to provide information about other potentially aggrieved persons (this "class" information will be included on the face of your charge).
- Counseled so that you will understand what to expect while your charge is being investigated.
- Counseled as to your rights, if any, under ADEA and EPA.
- Referred to the proper agency if your complaint cannot be handled by EEOC.

Review of Your Charge

After you have filed your charge, it will be reviewed by a senior manager to determine whether it should be assigned to a rapid charge unit or an extended unit, which conducts full-scale investigations, including onsite visits. An individual determination will be made on how your charge should be processed (even charges assigned to rapid charge processing units may be considered for more extensive investigations).

The Fact-finding Conference

After your charge has been filed, your employer will be notified that you have filed a charge of discrimination. Under Title VII, EEOC must notify your employer after receiving your charge. When the employer receives notification of the charge, the employer will normally be asked to come to EEOC for a fact-finding conference to discuss the allegations in your charge. You also will receive a copy of that notification.

The fact-finding conference is conducted by an EOS who is trained to conduct these conferences and to investigate employment discrimination charges. At the fact-finding conference, evidence will be presented by both you and your employer. Your employer will be asked to bring only those witnesses who have actual knowledge of the incident. Your witnesses will be interviewed prior to the conference. Only those people who have knowledge of the incident are permitted to speak at the conference.

Information obtained at the fact-finding conference will be used to help resolve your charge with a settlement satisfactory to both you and your employer. If settlement is impossible or inappropriate, your charge will be investigated further.

After the Conference

While most charges filed with EEOC are resolved without lengthy investigation, some charges require investigation beyond the fact-finding conference. If your charge is one of these, or if it is a charge which is not appropriate for a fact-finding conference, it will be investigated by either a rapid charge unit or an extended investigation unit.

Extended Investigation

If your charge is assigned for extended investigation at any stage following its receipt and is identified for possible litigation, it will be processed by a team that includes an attorney. The attorney will be involved in all critical decision points as the investigation proceeds and will work on the case from beginning to end. To the extent possible, extended investigations will include a visit to the facility in question.

Cause Determination

If the investigation shows that there is reasonable cause to believe that discrimination has occurred, the Commission will notify you and your employer of this decision. At this point, EEOC will being the conciliation efforts required under the statute.

No Cause Findings

If the Commission investigation concludes that there is no reasonable cause to believe that discrimination occurred, you and your employer will be notified of the findings. You have the right to request a review of the findings with EEOC in Washington, D.C. All appeal rights and instructions for filing a request for review will be sent to you along with the notification of findings. You will also be informed of your right to take your case to court if you choose.

Litigation

Most charges filed with EEOC, even those where the Commission decides to sue, are conciliated or settled before the case actually goes to trial. At all stages of the investigation, the Commission, as required by statute, will attempt to bring the matter to a resolution agreeable to all parties without costly litigation.

If, however, EEOC finds that there is reasonable cause to believe that discrimination has occurred and is unable to conciliate your charge, it will be considered by the Commission for possible litigation. If the Commission decides to litigate your case, a lawsuit will be filed in federal district court.

If the Commission decides not to litigate your case, a "right-to-sue" letter will be issued, which permits you to take your case to court, if you choose.

The State or Local Fair Employment Practices Agency

Title VII requires that the federal government defer charges of discrimination to a state or local agency if that agency meets certain criteria. EEOC has work-sharing agreements with many state or local agencies. Depending upon the agreement, your charge may be processed either by EEOC or the state agency. In any event, your employment discrimination charge will be handled under tight management and quality controls.

UNDER THE AGE DISCRIMINATION IN EMPLOYMENT ACT

(Age-Protects workers 40 years of age or older.)
During your initial contact with EEOC, you will be:

- Interviewed by an EOS who has been trained to handle age discrimination charges.
- Counseled as to your right to file either a charge or complaint.
- Interviewed about your allegations so that your charge may be properly written.
- Counseled as to your rights, if any, under Title VII.

If you decide to file a charge or complaint under ADEA:

- EEOC will investigate your charge/complaint.
- In the case of a charge, you and your employer may be asked to attend a fact-finding conference to discuss your charge.
- EEOC may initiate court action if a violation of the law is found and conciliation fails.

Private Suits

Individuals may file suit on their own behalf but not until 60 days after filing their charge of unlawful discrimination with EEOC and, where there is a state age discrimination law, with the state agency. Should EEOC take legal action, however, the individual may not file a private suit.

UNDER THE EQUAL PAY ACT

(Pay Difference Because of Sex)
During your initial contact with EEOC you will be:

- Interviewed by an EOS trained to handle equal pay discrimination complaints.
- Interviewed to determine if there is reason to believe that you have an equal pay discrimination complaint and to determine whether other individuals may also be affected.
- Counseled as to your rights, if any, under Title VII and ADEA.

Your complaint will be investigated on a sufficiently broad basis so that your identity will not be disclosed to your employer. If a violation of the law is found, EEOC will attempt to obtain appropriate prospective wage increases and back wages for all aggrieved individuals.

If the attempt to settle is not successful, the Commission may file suit to enforce the Act.

Private Suits

Under the Equal Pay Act, you have the right to file suit for backpay, liquidated damages, attorney's fees and court costs. However, you may not bring suit if you have been paid full back wages under supervision of the Commission or if the Commission has filed suit to collect the wages. A two-year statute of limitation applies to the recovery of unpaid wages, except in the case of willful violations, for which there is a three-year statute of limitation.

CONFIDENTIALITY

Under *Title VII*, except in unusual circumstances which will be discussed with you, your identity *must be* revealed.

Under *ADEA*, if you wish confidentiality you may file a *complaint* or have a charge filed on your behalf. The filing of a charge protects your right to file a private suit. If you file a *charge*, your name will be given to your employer.

Under *EPA*, EEOC will not disclose your identity without your written consent. However, if you elect to file a charge under *both* Title VII and EPA, your identity will be revealed.

RETALIATION

Under Title VII, ADEA, and EPA, employers are prohibited from retaliating against any employee who files a charge/complaint or participates in an EEOC investigation.

If an employer retaliates against an employee for filing a charge/complaint or for participating in an investigation, the Commission may ask for a Temporary Restraining Order which, if granted by the court, would prevent the employer from retaliating further.

ADDITIONAL INFORMATION

If you need further information, you may call EEOC toll free on 800-USA-EEOC. EEOC's TDD number (for the hearing impaired) is (202) 634-7057.

Appendix D

Filing an EEOC Charge/Complaint

Example

CHARGE OF DISCRIMINATION his form is affected by the Privacy Act of 1974; see Privacy Act Statement on reverse efore completing this form.		ENTER CHARGE NUMBER ☐ FEPA ☐ EEOC
__________________________ and EEOC *(State or local Agency, if any)*		
AME *(Indicate Mr., Ms., or Mrs.)*		HOME TELEPHONE NO. *(Include Area Code)*
TREET ADDRESS	CITY, STATE AND ZIP CODE	COUNTY
AMED IS THE EMPLOYER, LABOR ORGANIZATION, EMPLOYMENT AGENCY, APPRENTICESHIP COMMITTEE, TATE OR LOCAL GOVERNMENT AGENCY WHO DISCRIMINATED AGAINST ME *(If more than one list below.)*		
AME	NO. OF EMPLOYEES/MEMBERS	TELEPHONE NUMBER *(Include Area Code)*
TREET ADDRESS	CITY, STATE AND ZIP CODE	
AME		TELEPHONE NUMBER *(Include Area Code)*
TREET ADDRESS	CITY, STATE AND ZIP CODE	
AUSE OF DISCRIMINATION BASED ON *(Check appropriate box(es))* ☐ RACE ☐ COLOR ☐ SEX ☐ RELIGION ☐ NATIONAL ORIGIN ☐ AGE ☐ RETALIATION ☐ OTHER *(Specify)*		DATE MOST RECENT OR CONTINUING DISCRIMINATION TOOK PLACE *(Month, day, year)*
HE PARTICULARS ARE *(If additional space is needed, attached extra sheet(s)):*		
] I also want this charge filed with the EEOC. will advise the agencies if I change my address or telephone umber and I will cooperate fully with them in the processing my charge in accordance with their procedures.	NOTARY — (When necessary to meet State and Local Requirements) I swear to affirm that I have read the above charge and that it is true to the best of my knowledge, information and belief.	
declare under penalty of perjury that the foregoing is true nd correct. ate Charging Party *(Signature)*	SIGNATURE OF COMPLAINANT SUBSCRIBED AND SWORN TO BEFORE ME THIS DATE (Day, month, and year)	

Appendix E

Privacy Act Statement

(This form is covered by the Privacy Act of 1974, Public Law 93-579: Authority for requesting the personal data and the uses are given below.)

1. FORM NUMBER/TITLE/DATE. EEOC Form 5, CHARGE OF DISCRIMINATION, March 1984.

2. AUTHORITY. 42 U.S.C.§ 2000e-5(b), 29 U.S.C.§ 211, 29 U.S.C.§ 626.

3. PRINCIPAL PURPOSE(S). The purpose of the charge, whether recorded initially on this form or in some other way reduced to writing and later re-

corded on this form, is to invoke the jurisdiction of the Commission.

4. ROUTINE USES. This form is used to determine the existence of facts which fall within the Commission's jurisdiction to investigate, determine, conciliate and litigate charges of unlawful employment practices. Information provided on this form will be used by Commission employees to guide the Commission's investigatory activities. This form may be disclosed to other State, local and federal agencies as may be appropriate or necessary to carrying out the Commission's functions. A copy of this charge will ordinarily be served upon the person against whom the charge is made.

5. WHETHER DISCLOSURE IS MANDATORY OR VOLUNTARY AND EFFECT ON INDIVIDUAL FOR NOT PROVIDING INFORMATION. Charges must be in writing and should identify the parties and action or policy complained of. Failure to have a charge which identifies the parties in writing may result in the Commission not accepting the charge. Charges under Title VII must be sworn to or affirmed. Charges under the ADEA should ordinarily be signed. Charges may be clarified or amplified later by amendment. It is not mandatory that this form be used to provide the requested information.

6. [ ] Under Section 706 of Title VII of the Civil Rights Act of 1964, as amended, this charge will be deferred to and will be processed by the State or local agency indicated. Upon completion of the agency's processing, you will be notified of its final

resolution in your case. If you wish EEOC to give Substantial Weight Review to the agency's findings, you must send us a request to do so, in writing, within fifteen (15) days of your receipt of the agency's finding. Otherwise, we will adopt the agency's finding as EEOC's and close your case.

NOTICE OF NON-RETALIATION REQUIREMENTS

Section 704(a) of the Civil Rights Act of 1964, as amended, and Section 4(d) of the Age Discrimination in Employment Act of 1967, as amended, state:

It shall be an unlawful employment practice for an employer to discriminate against any of his employees or applicants for employment, for an employment agency to discriminate against any individual, or for a labor organization to discriminate against any member thereof or applicant for membership, because he has opposed a practice made an unlawful employment practice by this title or because he has made a charge, testified, assisted, or participated in any manner in an investigation, proceeding, or hearing under this title.

The Equal Pay Act of 1963 contains similar provisions. Persons filing charges of discrimination are advised of these Non-Retaliation Requirements and are instructed to notify EEOC if any attempt at retaliation is made.

Index

T

U

V

W

X